The Bigger Picture

One Man's Journey from Religious Fundamentalism to Reality

By

Colin Setterfield

The Bigger Picture

Copyright © 2019 Colin Setterfield

ALL RIGHTS RESERVED

No part of this ebook may be reproduced or transmitted in any form or by any means, electronic or mechanical, including photocopying, without the the written permission of the author.

This ebook is a work of nonfiction. Some of the names of characters, organizations and places have been changed to protect the identities of those involved.

ISBN 978-1-988719-17-7

Colin Setterfield

Table of Contents

Introduction
1: Developing a Concept of God
2: Salvation
3: Trouble in Paradise
4: A New Job Opportunity
5: Never a Dull Moment
6: An Unexpected Promotion
7: A Touch of the Miraculous
8: A Change of Ownership
9: My First Commission
10: Sorry, My Mistake
11: A Brief Interlude
12: A New Horizon
13: A Mandate for Children's Education
14: A Sticky Situation
15: Hold Onto That Calling
16: Categories of Christian Believers
17: The Prosperous Image Perception
18: The Combination of Two Fellowships
19: The Ups and the Downs
20: Mrs. Promiscuous
21: Moving On
22: Immigration
23: My Greatest Mistake
24: God's Response to Our Dilemmas
25: Some Unexpected Help
26: Dodging a Bullet
27: Jumping Churches Again
28: Divine Inspiration?
29: Starting Another Church? Really?
30: Gaining Some Influential Members
31: The Ebb and Flow of Membership
32: An Awkward Confrontation
33: Music Group Mutiny

The Bigger Picture

34: Picking up the Pieces
35: Reflection on a Past Event
36: DR Theory
37: The End of a Long Road
38: Entertaining the Possibilities of the Bigger Picture
39: Considering the Possibilities
40: Back to Secular Life
Notes

Colin Setterfield

A Cynical Perspective

A missionary thought to have drowned in a shipwreck is discovered ten years later on an island. His rescuers noticed two roughly constructed abodes above the shore line.

Rescuer: "What is the purpose of that abode on the left for?"

Missionary: "That's my church."

Rescuer: "What is the purpose of the abode on the right?"

Missionary: "Oh, that's the church I used to go to."

Introduction

Before I started on this book, the relegation of my personal life to the printed page threatened me on many levels. With more than three decades of church involvement as a leader and preacher in the body of Christ, a tenure that includes nineteen years of full-time ministry, people had come to see me as a steadfast spiritual leader and teacher who never wavered in his Christian duties. It may now appear to some that I have turned away from my core beliefs, but such a conclusion provides little justice for the paradigm shift in my belief system. What I believe has happened is a transition in perspective with regard to the interpretation of the source information.

The mention of several negative experiences throughout the time of my ministry might produce the impression that this book is written from a position of bitterness and because of this particular concern, I've shelved the story several times, to make sure that all the negative feelings and emotions experienced throughout the time of my ministerial service have been dealt with. The passage of time lends new perspective and it took several years of soul-searching to deal with the betrayal that led me down the rocky path toward near self-destruction. I can now say with conviction that without these negative experiences in my life, it would not have been possible for me to see the bigger picture, which I present as a part of this story.

*

All the belief systems that stem from the time of the Sumerian1 civilization[1], up to the present day, paint pictures that tend to ignore the dynamic truths of the real world around us. These beliefs tend to separate their advocates into polarized groups that lead to separate pursuits of spiritual truth. Because of human nature, people have sought ways to confirm their truth as Absolute. When the real truth of our interconnectedness and singular mind earns its place in our hearts, we will see that all the great religions of the world basically point to the same truth about the Creator and eternal issues. This epiphany leads to a grounded belief system rooted in our observable reality. I believe anyone who can see the bigger picture will realize that all religious beliefs should mature into a guide that advocates love, tolerance, and understanding. Such a perspective will move the world into an era of universal peace.

My story is not unique or profound. The questions conceived in my mind with regard to the Creator are the same for everyone, and I have no claim to fame or originality, with one caveat: my story is hereby publicized for the reader, to accept and enjoy, or to reject with or without prejudice. Anyone who reads this book, may be in search of a greater sense of reality in their own belief system—or it may be that they seek something to debate. If the latter is the motive, I suggest that before continuing, they ask themselves a few honest questions: Are they happy with what they believe? Would adding a greater sense of reality to their belief system be something they might explore? Are they able to read about alternatives to life's story without prejudice? And perhaps the most important question of all: Are they one hundred percent sure they have found the ABSOLUTE TRUTH?

I'll cut to the chase: Only the Creator knows the absolute truth, but there is a viable alternative to mainstream, traditional religious belief systems. The bigger picture incorporates real-world scientific discovery and combines it with the innate sense of creation theory that many people already possess. In essence, I believe there is one step beyond religious belief, a step toward the bigger picture: REALITY[2.]

This step is for those who desire to know the Creator in a deeper way: a way that incorporates an awareness of the universe we live in. The good news: it really doesn't matter whether you take this step or not. because the question of "final destinations" is not linked to what you believe. The bigger picture will help you see the cosmos and all its creatures in a different light. It will help you find your purpose and connectedness to the universe, and free you from the bondage religions, by interpretation of scripture, can impose on the human psyche. It is not wrong to be religious, if by that definition a person is in sync with their habitat, environment, and relationships to a degree that does not impinge on the beliefs and rights of others. Taking the extra step toward reality will, however, create a pathway to the type of freedom Jesus referred to: You will know the truth, and the truth will set you free.

DISCLOSURE: To protect the privacies of the people involved in this story, the author has changed many (but not all) of the names of those involved. The cities or towns where the author's ministry took place are also not mentioned, but the author confirms that all circumstances and experiences listed are genuine and true. The intents and actions of people involved reflect the author's opinions and are not intended as any form of indictment against any particular person or interpretation of ancient scripture; it is the author's story and he tells it as it happened.

The Bigger Picture

1: Developing a Concept of God

As a young child, I enjoyed the good fortune to have been raised on a farm. My father, a lecturer at a technical institute, hobby-farmed chickens and mushrooms on a fifty-acre country lot situated about 13 miles outside the city of Pretoria, the capital of the South Africa.**3** In 1961 the government changed the country's status from a Union to that of a Republic, followed by the more recent change of regime in 1994.

The rugged nature of the terrain allowed me to spend many happy hours in exploration of the nooks and crannies offered by the bush and tree-infested hillocks, many which received an appropriate name, the product of a little boy's active imagination. I could hide in dozens of places and never be found—not that I ever had a reason to not be found.

My brother Robert, eight years older and my nemesis at the time, took great delight in telling me frightening stories about what went on during the night-hours on the farm. In particular, he insisted that a certain outcrop called Ghost Rock, held the skeletons of long departed occupants of our area. These rocks, shaped like long flat slabs, looked like the ancient sarcophaguses found in Egyptian tombs and Robert told me that the ghosts popped out of the graves and danced on them in the midnight hours.

Five years old and terrified of Ghost Rock I made sure to give the area a wide birth from that time onward. After that story, however, ghosts became as real to me as live people and the narrative imprinted itself on my juvenile mind as an undeniable truth. As the years passed by I realized that ghosts, mere figments of my imagination, could not harm me in any way. The use of imagination is often a way we give substance to concepts undetectable by the physical senses and is common to all of us. Parents teach their children imaginary concepts at a young age, like Santa, the tooth fairy, and goblins. We soon realize that these imaginary characters stem from stories and myth, passed on to us by our forebears.

Perhaps the intention of these stories is to help us judge between reality and fantasy; to help the young mind develop a power of imagination that will lead to a healthy pursuit of truth. Perhaps there is a narrow line between imagination and faith. I believe the power of imagination plays a great part in the establishment of our various belief systems and, most important of all, a concept of the Creator of our Universe.**4**

One other rock on the farm deserves to be mentioned at this juncture of my story: perched on one of the farm's several hillocks it overlooked the long drive up to the farmhouse from the gate. Because of the rock's size and shape my brother and I named it "God's Rock". A flat spot on top provided a safe viewpoint from where we inspected the world below us and I often sat there in contemplation of the issues of life. Although young and adventurous, I displayed a melancholic temperament which would have me seek out the solitude of this rock, where I could be alone with my thoughts. More often than not, those thoughts turned to the awareness of an entity much greater than my own mind. I attempted to derive a feasible concept of the Creator. I thought it would be great to meet Him if He might come down from His domain in the sky and settle some of my burning questions. I imagined this great God in human form, beside me on the rock, with the two of us engaged in earnest conversation about life. I posited how advantageous it would be to His reputation (and my own childlike sense of justice) if He might cause a certain slipper (with which my mother applied much-deserved discipline to my posterior during times of my disobedience), to disappear.

There are no limits to imagination. I do remember a "warm and fuzzy" at the time, and entertained that one day, I would indeed meet this God.

Fear, after love, is perhaps the most prominent emotion a young child will experience in life. Fear and imagination go hand-in-hand, and I am amazed at how quickly one's security can be disturbed when these two partners get together. I love my older brother, Robert, but he became instrumental in the instillation of an unhealthy fear of the dark into my heart. Even prior to the story of Ghost Rock, he frightened me every night at bedtime. The farmhouse, built in 1945, provided our family with three bedrooms, one, which became my dad's office. This meant that Robert and I shared a bedroom for six years until my father decided that Robert needed his own.

Many a night, while in his bed near the windows, Robert would knock and scrape on the wall and follow it with gasps of fear. Then he whispered my name in a muted, but audible voice. "Conky?" (my nickname). "Can you see it? There at the door? It wants to come in—it's going to eat us!"

Often he turned off the bedroom light, jumped into his bed, and moaned in feigned fear of some terrible monster at the door. I would grip the side of my mattress in terror and hold on for dear life, just in case the apparition came and tried to carry me off. Once Robert sat upright in bed, threw his pillow at the entrance, and shouted a curse, all a wicked ruse to instill more fear into my terrified soul. The screams of fear brought my parents on the run from the sitting room where they had been reading. My mother often scolded Robert in a gentle voice.

"Robert, please stop frightening your little brother," and then she always follow it with, "AND COLIN, STOP YOUR CRYING; ONLY BABIES CRY."

The Bigger Picture

One night, my parents visited friends in the city to play contract bridge and left us to our own devices. Robert, almost a teenager, took charge of me with implicit instructions to make sure I bathed and went to bed at an appropriate time. This night is forever etched in my memory. The rain poured for several hours in the early evening, and the sound of rolling thunder seemed to shake the very foundations of the house. Lightning, with brilliant, intermittent flashes of blue and purple, lit up the night sky outside like a fireworks display. By the time darkness fell, I feared the lights might be knocked out, an event which often took place during electrical storms. The time came for me to make ready for bed, and His Royal Wickedness ordered me to leave the sitting room for the journey to the bathroom, situated at the other end of the building.

The passageway, which serviced the bedrooms and bathroom, possessed a singe overhead light that could be operated by separate switches, one at each end—a very modern inclusion in the electrics of the day. This arrangement stoked the fires of Robert's imagination as he ordered me, with my mind already in a state of fear, to go and run the bathwater. Unbeknown to me, he entertained a vile plan that must have been in percolation on the back-burner of his devious mind for some time. When I reached the far end of the passage I stopped to contemplate the possibility of ghosts gathered in the darkness of my parent's bedroom to the left, and in the adjacent bathroom to my right.

To reach up and turn on the bathroom light posed another problem not anticipated. I could not reach the light switch, even on tip-toe, and with my arm at maximum stretch. I yelled for my brother to come to my aid. Robert stuck his head around the corner at the bottom end of the passage and let rip with the most hideous, maniacal laugh. I froze in time and space. I wanted to scream with fear, but my voice would not cooperate. That's when he did the unthinkable: he turned the corridor light off via the switch at his end and the entire area around me plunged into darkness. Only soft light from the sitting room permeated through from the distant end, and I stood immobile below the unreachable switch above my head. With sudden volition, the imaginary hands of demons and ghosts from Ghost Rock clutched at my soul. I soiled myself and collapsed in tears.

Robert's merciless reign of terror never seemed to attract much attention from my parents, who thought it amusing. At times Robert and I got on well and played many rambunctious games. Our imaginations ran rampant as we played out scenes from films seen at the local cinema. Each month-end my dad treated the family to a night at one of the movies in Pretoria.

All in all, life on the farm produced an idyllic fantasy of adventure despite interspersed moments of trepidation and terror. Fear of the dark continued to haunt me every night, even after Robert's departure to his own bedroom. A section of the mattress on the side of my bed that faced the wall suffered where my

The Bigger Picture

hand tightly held it for the years of my early youth. Other factors, caused by an over-active imagination, added to my terror and in time a nightmare developed in which the front door would start to open as I arrived in the entrance hall. Some outside force acted against my limited strength as I tried to close the door and each time the force won the contest. The nightmare ended abruptly at this point, to leave me wide awake and in a cold sweat. Sometimes it would be the kitchen door and other times the sliding door in the dining room which led to an outside verandah.

One day (later in life) I managed to figure out the reason for the development of this nightmare. The lock on the dining room's sliding door never worked from the day of installation, and my dad who worked his full-time job at the college plus the management of the mushroom and chicken business on weekends, never found the time to repair it. Our dog, a boerbull, slept outside in front of the door to discourage any would-be intruders. Despite the eventual rectification of the lock problem, the nightmare continued to weigh into my adult years.

A short while after my tenth birthday my parents, motivated by financial circumstances, decided to move away from the farm to occupy a rental home in the city of Pretoria; and for several years, we lived in a suburb called Clydesdale. In July 1957, after the farm's tenants did a midnight flit, my parents decided to move back there to protect the investment and it pleased me to be back in my domain again. This tenure of occupation, however, did not last long. Due to my father's successful job application for the principalship of a high school[5] in the coastal city of Durban we pulled up roots once again and moved to the province of Natal. My brother, Robert, after his graduation from university, took a job with the country's largest steel producer in a fast-growing Transvaal city and for the twenty years that followed, we rarely saw each other.

Moments before we left the farm for the last time, I knelt down and kissed the ground. The old windmill, situated on a borehole at the bottom of the kopje on which the house stood, stared back at me in solemn farewell, and I remember the sting of tears as they bubbled from my eyes. Even today, when I close my eyes and think of that final goodbye, I can see the scene with clarity.

We moved away from the farm in January 1960, and many years passed before I saw it again.

2: Salvation

I met my wife-to-be, Adeline, in October 1964—a most fortuitous and influential event that placed my life on a path of greater stability. Before our marriage in March 1967, we attended several counseling sessions with the Reverend Doctor Andre de Villiers of the Durban, Frere Road, Presbyterian Church. At the time, I worked shifts at an oil refinery in Reunion on the outskirts of Durban and because of work constraints Adeline and I attended separate counseling sessions. In the church office I remember the sight of all the degrees and diplomas which hung on the wall behind the desk and thought to myself what a cushy job this man enjoyed. I never realized at the time I would find myself in a similar position one day.

After the completion of my military conscription[6], we settled down in Durban to make a life, and in April 1969, celebrated the birth of our daughter, Alison. A few traumatic, but happy growth years followed as we juggled jobs, raised a child, and attempted to maintain good social relationships with our friends. One day, a delicate situation arose between Adeline and my mother as the latter believed our daughter suffered neglect. My mother's perception of child-rearing, rooted in a bygone era when mothers stayed at home and fathers went out to work, had long since fallen out of vogue. Our current reality at the time required a financial contribution from both parents in order to come by so I arranged for Alison to be with a caregiver during the day. My mother, bless her soul, felt that she needed to do something about the status quo. My new job as maintenance manager for a swimming pool construction company, a short walk from our flat, meant that Adeline could use the car to get to her place of employment downtown while I carried little Alison in my arms to the childcare facility, on my way to work. Every work-day morning produced a heart-wrenching moment when mother and daughter separated, with added trauma when I handed Alison over to her caregiver.

My mother arrived at our home one Saturday morning to confront my wife about our daughter's care. An argument ensued between them after which my mother removed Alison from the flat and carried her off. My upset wife called me at work to share the status quo. I, in turn, called my Dad at the college to make my annoyance known and then went straight to my parents' flat to rescue my daughter. After a while matters settled down, but things remained strained between my mother and I. At the end of that year we made a decision to move away from Durban to a small Northern Natal community, the home of Adeline's sister, Annette, and her husband, George, who offered me a work opportunity with his farm-dam building enterprise.

The Bigger Picture

The emotional turbulence of the times, given the "abduction" episode and resignation from of our regular jobs, plus a move to a new area, placed a heavy strain on our marriage but we soldiered through. I decided to start my own swimming pool company in conjunction with the farm-dam concern while Adeline worked for the local municipality. We found day-care for Alison and started a new chapter in our lives. George and Annette moved down to a small community outside Pietermaritzburg to open up another section of his business, which allowed us to move into their vacant home. I also took over one of George's old trucks for my swimming pool endeavor.[7] Things went a bit awry for both of us, however. The country's economy took a nosedive and interest rates skyrocketed; business ventures became risky and credit fell into short supply. After building one pool, I could not get any new contracts; and George's market also shrank to the point where he laid off the second dam-building team, the one under my control in the rural districts of our community. Financially, this state of affairs left me high and dry and I had no option but to find a job.

With all the insecurity and our financial future in some doubt Adeline and I became susceptible to religion. Two other couples, new-found friends who attended different denominational churches, came to our rescue.

The one couple, whom I will call Godfrey and Olivia, invited us to their home on several occasions, and we ended up one

Sunday evening at a service in their church, an Afrikaans[8] branch of what I will call "The Word of God Church." Due to a lack of English-speaking congregants in the town, the Afrikaans branch did its best to be as bilingual as possible. Adeline and I, both at a low point, gave our lives over to the Lord and accepted Jesus as our savior in the first meeting we attended. The pastor, a young married man, only two years older than I, took me on as a project; and thus began my long dance with a fundamentalist, conservative, evangelical belief system.[9]

The rules for congregant women focused on the use of as little make-up as possible, dresses with hems below the knees, and hats to serve as head coverings. The men wore suits of a conservative cut and dark color, with white shirts and ties that matched. The eldership did not tolerate any modern fads in dress, and even considered sport, although not outlawed, to be a worldly practice. Godfrey and I did, however, play badminton at the local club.

After the closure of my business, I took a job as the manager of a men's clothing store. This, together with Adeline's job, helped us pay the bills; and suddenly, I fell in love with this new religious life. In 1972, Adeline gave birth to identical twin boys, Paul and Andrew; and for a while, we needed to focus on seeing them through the initial months of child rearing, which took much from our church attendance. But I found ways to stay as involved as possible.

The Bigger Picture

It did not occur to me at the time that the strict church rules bordered on cultish practice and life in the Spirit became my main focus, much to Adeline's chagrin, as she tended to be more reserved. After the initial shock of the twins, I threw myself headlong into every semblance of belief the church advocated. My life appeared to be on an upward trend for the first time since the Durban days, and doctrine appeared to an area I could get my teeth into. Within a short period of time the pastor began to lean on me as his right-hand man. This did not mean any high-level church position such as a deacon or an elder at the time; but I did become the youth leader, and after six months preached my first sermon to the youth members. Six months later, I became a regular lay preacher in the church and often took meetings in the pastor's absence.

One evening, Godfrey took me aside to suggest that I seek the baptism in the Holy Spirit. Up to this point, Adeline and I had considered baptism in water—usually the first step that followed salvation, in accordance with tradition—but Godfrey opined that the order of the events did not matter. The Baptism in the Spirit imparted certain spiritual gifts for greater power to lead an exemplary life.

Godfrey prayed over me as we sat alone in the church on one of the pews. In the dark, only the moonlight filtered through the windows to illuminate the pews and piano while Godfrey hovered over me with his hands on my shoulders. I listened careful-ly to his speaking in tongues and when he asked me to speak out the words that came into my mind, even if I felt they seemed to be gibberish, I complied. My whole body reacted to the excitement of the moment. The strong mental concentration caused me to fall into a trance-like state, and my muscles felt as though a strong force had taken hold of them. I stammered out a whole bunch of meaningless words for several minutes, and when it ended, I felt drained but excited. Godfrey explained how this experience often took place in early biblical times, and served to empower the church in their work amongst the unbelievers. After a prolonged absence of hundreds of years it appeared again, amongst the Quakers[10] after the spiritual renaissance in the 1600s.

The practice of speaking in other tongues, interpretation, and prophecy became the subject of the meetings, and I can remember a few loud worship services where the men prayed out loudly in the vernacular. The few English-speaking congregants always used King James English[11] to enforce the authority of their thoughts, while the women wailed and chanted like banshees. Adeline hated this, but I just took it all in my stride. Kudos to my beautiful wife for sticking by me through thick and thin! The church started to play a huge role in every facet of our lives, with the Bible becoming the go-to source for all situations. I did not realize what a profound and negative impact this lifestyle would have on the lives of my family. With the children too young to be constantly taken out at night, Adeline soon became a "church widow". She stayed at home with them while I attended the meetings. My need to keep up my religious profile in the eyes of the congregation appeared to be the greatest motivation for this steadfast commitment. This is an aspect I greatly regret, and despite my family's eventual forgiveness of my shortcomings, the scars left on their lives lie close under the surface.

I became so blinded by my own spiritual ambition I could not see the effects suffered by my family at the time. The anticipated road ahead with the eventual career goal of full-time ministry, filled me with expectation and I surged on regardless of the potential family repercussions. A ministerial course through the medium of correspondence with a Gospel Bible College in Pretoria followed and my time became divided between study, church meetings, and a day job—which left little time for family.

Trouble, however, stalked our church and difficult times lay ahead.

3: Trouble in Paradise

Due to the church's education curriculum, reinforced by the interaction and experiences from social visits, a quick spiritual growth followed our initial introduction to church life. Events, some amusing and some not, come to mind as I write this manuscript. A middle-aged couple, Neil and Joy Parker and longtime members of the church, lived with their five children in a home that backed onto the rear of our property. Joy, a large rotund lady with a high-pitched laugh, possessed a heart of gold; and Neil, a laborer, lacked the education to make any advance in his status or income. Everyone knew Neil to be the bluntest knife in the drawer, and his knowledge of Christian values appeared shaky, to say the least.

During times of worship, he would often speak in tongues—a sound that resembled an animal in extreme distress, followed by a step out into the aisle to fall over backward in a trance. It happened time and again until people started to roll their eyes in expectation of his outbursts. The smaller children stared at Neil and cast nervous glances at their parents, who caught each other's eyes in acknowledgment of the man's obvious misdirected enthusiasm.

The Bigger Picture

Neil, often out of work due to his lack of mental capacity, did garden work at the church to pass the time and kind-hearted members of the congregation helped his family financially whenever they could. Joy, bless her heart, knew all her husband's short-comings, but loved the man in spite of it. She baked delicious pastries which were brought to the church for the after-service refreshment time as if doing penance for him. I remember one time, after a long bout of joblessness, Neil appeared in his backyard early one morning with a rolled-up blueprint tucked under one arm, and a bright yellow construction hardhat perched on his head: his application for a job with a local construction company appeared to have materialized and he wanted all the neighbors to know about it. Adeline laughed when I commented that he must have pulled the wool over his new boss's eyes to part with official drawings, because Neil would certainly not have known how to read them. The job lasted about one day.

Many strange things happened in those first three years. A business owner and a longtime member of the congregation became involved with the church organist and they carried on an illicit affair until the business owner's wife discovered her husband's shenanigans. We all wondered what she saw in him, a rough man with a pock-marked face and a foul mouth, not a great catch for any woman. I could only imagine that life at home presented a challenge for the organist as her non-Christian husband hated the church. A woman who fell into sin with a married man, both members of another congregation in a time gone by, fell into disrepute and left her church to seek membership with the Church of God. Our church placed her under an extreme form of discipline, extracted a vocal repentance for the evil deed and several years later the disciplinary regime ended. A short while after that she fell in love with a much younger, single man in our congregation. This sparked some very lively discussions amongst the congregants as to the chastity of the situation. The young man's parents vented their fears to anyone who would listen. The couple ended up getting married after a very short courtship, but the tongues of the congregants wagged so furiously that the couple decided to leave the church in order to keep the peace.

Another, disturbing incident took place on a Sunday night in the winter of 1972. The pastor, about to close the meeting with prayer, looked up in surprise as several loud bangs emanated from the street outside. He garbled a short prayer to end the meeting and everyone rushed outside to witness the spectacle. A car raced off down the road, and it became apparent that the driver of the vehicle struck several of the congregants' cars parked on the verge. Our rough business owner, the one with the pock-marked face, grabbed a friend, and the two of them jumped into his truck in hot pursuit. About thirty minutes later, as we started to leave for home, the two men returned with huge smiles on their faces.

"The bastards were drunk, and as we rounded the corner at the bottom of the road, we found the car on its roof in the ditch!"

"What did you do?" asked the pastor.

Pockmark grinned. "There were two black men, so we pulled them both out of the wreck and beat them to a pulp."

I could see the horrified look on the pastor's face. "Did you check to see if they were injured?"

Pockmark's accomplice answered the question. "Of course not. They are blacks; we gave them what they deserved, then dropped them off at the local police station and laid a charge."

I remembered the shocked looks on the faces of the few congregants who still remained. Even the church harbored elements of racial discrimination.

About two years after our introduction to the church, the congregation passed through a period of crisis where certain members in leadership polarized with the congregants—my first taste of "real church politics." The pastor, accused of heresy by several of the elders in the congregation because he favored the doctrine of Eternal Security,[12] found himself in trouble with the denominational leaders of the group.

Two of the church elders of an Armenian background vehemently opposed this doctrine. They believed that salvation could be lost if one participated in sinful acts, whereas "Eternal Securists" believed salvation could not be forfeited under any circumstance. No one could to see their way around this matter, and people started to leave because of the infighting. It upset me, because my friends Godfrey and Olivia decided to move to another church and the pastor, my greatest ally, for the sake of his own peace decided to take up a calling in another city; and for months after that, a battle raged between the elders. The atmosphere in the meetings changed from lively, loving participation to a subdued sullen worship as a new challenge arose in the wake of the departed pastor: an electoral procedure (called an electoral college) to decide on a new shepherd for the congregation.

Some weeks later, a young man and recent graduate of the Bible school in Pretoria, who married weeks before he responded to our call, took the post advertised with our denominations head office. Thrown into this quagmire of rivalry, I could only imagine how hard this must have been for the new pastor and his young bride. I quickly established a rapport with him, and we became good friends. The church continued on its destructive path, however, and matters became so strained that after several more months of struggle with the status quo, Adeline and I decided to leave the Word of God Church. I lost all faith in the new pastor's ability to stabilize the wreck; to leave appeared the only way out of what had become, for us, an intolerable situation. I looked to the only other Pentecostal[13] church in the town—the church that our friends, Godfrey and Olivia, now attended. Due to the fact that they had left the church for another denomination, our elders deemed them to have fallen away[14] from the faith and discouraged the congregants from any form of contact with the deserters. We, on the other hand, glad to renew our friendship with Godfrey and Olivia, entertained few regrets with regard to our apparent apostasy. It could only be imagined what the Word of God elders, in the wake of our departure, said about us.

Godfrey shared a fragment of history about our new place of fellowship, The Assembly of True believers: Before they joined with the Word of God Church The Assembly hosted the initial attraction to spiritual matters before a nasty split between the elders shattered their confidence in the fellowship. At the time, The Assembly of True Believers and the Word of God Church provided the sole options for the Pentecostal style of worship and relevant doctrines. The Assemblies, however, did not support a bi-lingual language delivery; but nevertheless, the two churches traded off their "fallen away" congregants to each other. As Pentecostal, evangelical fundamentalists we never considered any of the mainline denominations, such as Anglican, Presbyterian, Methodist, or Baptist as potential spiritual homes. According to our elders, none of these denominations preached the "real" truth (i.e., they did not preach the baptism in the Holy Spirit and the speaking in other tongues). To us, they fared no better than the heathen.

Despite these negative connotations, I remember many times of great fellowship, moments of epiphany and spiritual fulfillment, experiences that would later help me to hone my personal service in the Lord's work. I considered myself to be one of the chosen,[15] with a gift to preach and teach God's Word. It took me many years to discover the truth about organized religion, and such typical and exclusive gatherings of people who promoted the idealistic belief of there being only one right way; the problem I failed to understand lay in the exclusive attitude our special ideals placed on all other religions, plus many of the other denominations within the Christian realm.

The one aspect of human nature that runs jointly with agreement is disagreement. The platform of opinion rides high on the back of doctrinal interpretations; and when there is disagreement it is settled by the expulsion of dissenters or a split in the congregation. At the time I did not realize the extent of this problem—most churches endured a corridor of crisis at least every three years after original establishment in a community. There are, of course, exceptions to this rule.

The Biblical adage of "Can two walk together unless they agree?", Amos 3:3, is the way Christians justify a break in their spiritual ranks. I myself believed this justification during my tenure in full-time ministry, and found consolation in the thought that God allowed these splits in order to increase the platforms for the purpose of evangelical witness. A church that splits will form two different bodies of people, and eventually the impact of the split will be swallowed up by the recruitment of more new members. The truth, however, is that many lives are shattered, with some leaving the Body of Christ forever and some carrying spiritual wounds that are never healed. Doctrinal differences forged by the opinions of men are the main reasons for the many different denominations that surfaced after the Reformation.

As fundamentalists, we think our primal instincts change because we say the right words in a moment of penitence. Our deep-rooted bias, constructed by our first impressions or the teachings with which we first bonded, lie close beneath the surface and often guide the decisions we make. A lack of tolerance of opinion lies at the very root of all religious fundamentalism, because teachings are seen as sacred and are taught as "absolute truth." Therefore, anyone who disagrees with a particular group's laid-down path to divinity is accused of not walking in the full light of God's word. What people fail to comprehend in all this is that the truth, in human terms, is in a very subjective form, and is influenced by one's point of view, personality, cultural background, and initial teaching. Human truth can only, at best, be described as the result of the human mind making an attempt to understand the things of the Spirit. Only the Creator has the absolute truth.

4: A New Job Opportunity

Our move to the Assembly of True Believer's Fellowship, filled with rich experiences and opportunities for me to preach, came as a breath of fresh air. The fundamental issues of doctrine between our old church and the new place of worship remained similar, with some small differences; and for a while, we thrived under the ministry of the pastoral couple in charge.

In June 1974, I managed to get a job with a large appliance manufacturer as a learner Work Study[16] Officer. The field of Work Study featured with some prominence in the factory economics of those days, and with work in short supply, I felt fortunate to get the job. It entailed the provision of organized time studies for parts manufactured on the factory floor and related to the establishment of labor costs. I believed that the opportunity came from God, so with so much to learn, I threw myself headlong into the work.

*

Piet Van Heerden

Work at the factory came with a downside which manifested as my personal cross to bear for the two years that followed. Piet Van Heerden, head of the Work Study department, and a member of the Dutch Reformed denomination, (the institution dubbed as South Africa's "state church"), became my new boss. The majority of the ruling political party[17] officials aligned themselves with this church group. Piet, refused to talk English, so it fell to me to converse with him in his home language, Afrikaans. He taught me everything about time studies and calculations, which served up the main labor component of man-hours for the costing department. I recall his first question at my initial interview.

"What church do you belong to?"

He gave me a stony stare when I told him Adeline and I held membership with the Assembly of True Believers Fellowship. For a moment I thought the interview would come to a swift end, because The State Church looked upon both the Assemblies Fellowship and the Word of God Church as sects. The general manager of the company, however, did not have such considerations, and I believe this got me the job. Piet informed me I needed to embark on the study of an Engineering Qualification to secure my long-term employment with the company. He shared details of his own personal commitment to such an avenue of study and suggested a correspondence course through the Wit-

The Bigger Picture

watersrand Technical College in Johannesburg, which would help me make up time if I worked hard. We would then both graduate in three years. This, of course, placed an extra pressure on my family and church involvement, but I desired to establish a permanent career, so I agreed.

One year after I joined the company, Piet fell off the wagon. His problem with alcohol took everyone by surprise and posed a problem for our general manager who after some deliberation decided to give Piet the opportunity to consider a rehabilitation solution. If Piet "dried out" over the course of the two-week program offered by a Pretoria institution he could have his job back. The manager made it clear that should Piet refuse such treatment his job would be forfeited.

"He is actually quite brilliant, and such a good worker," said the manager. "Everyone deserves a second chance."

The general manger spoke to Piet's wife who confessed that Piet's "binge alcoholism" allowed him to stay on the wagon for long stretches, but given a short period of stress, circumstances sometimes overwhelm him and send him off on a drinking spree. The general manager asked me to drive Piet to the rehabilitation center outside Pretoria, some 250 kilometers away, where he could receive the relevant treatment. I agreed to use my own car and later received reimbursement for gas used. Piet's wife agreed to accompany us for the facilitation of her husband's admission into the clinic and on my arrival at Piet's home, it shocked me to see the awful change in his demeanor. He swore at his wife, called her all sorts of derogatory names, and could not stand up or walk without assistance. We managed to bundle him into the back of the car and took off for Pretoria.

Piet's wife, an attractive brunette in her forties, ignored his outbursts and appeared to take everything in her stride. She told me that her husband's relapses occurred at least once every three years. The family couldn't afford unemployed, because without his income the family would be destitute. With two teenagers in high school and a mortgage to pay the constant fear of his problem hung like the sword of Damocles over their heads. Piet insisted after their marriage that his wife be a stay-at-home mom, and she therefore possessed no job skills. This placed her at a tremendous disadvantage, because few jobs existed in our town that, if she decided to break away, would pay her enough to support herself and the children. I soon discovered that because of Piet's insobriety, she no longer possessed any faith in God. This, of course, put me into witness mode, and we chatted for the next hour about things of faith until I heard Piet stir in the seat behind me. The backseat, not quite wide enough to accommodate Piet's, horizontal frame, meant that he lay squashed in a fetal position with head cranked at an angle against one rear door.

I kept to the maximum allowable speed limit of 120 kms per hour and continued to listen to Piet's wife prattle on about her

The Bigger Picture

children when in an instant I felt my head jerk upwards under pressure from two powerful hands clamped around my throat from behind. My last recollection of the road ahead confirmed it to be straight, without any bends, and the verges on each side wide enough for a vehicle to pull over for a quick stop. Piet, in marginal relief from his stupor, must have thought me to be one of the demons in his dream. His grasp around my throat made it impossible for me to look anywhere else but at the ceiling. Piet's wife turned in the seat beside me and started to beat at his hands and slap him in the face. His drunken slurs and grunts lessened as she shouted at him to let go of my neck while I braked the vehicle to a lower speed. I needed to edge over onto the verge and bring my car to a safe stop. An oncoming car flashed by at speed, the driver unconscious of the potential disaster as the crunch of gravel under the tires, sounded in my ears.

As we came to a stop, Piet let go of my neck and fell back into the fetal position again. Shaken, both his wife and I climbed out of the vehicle to stare up and down the freeway and then at each other, both shocked at the closeness of the call.

Later that afternoon, we drove into the clinic's driveway. I helped Piet out of the car, and we supported him into the waiting room where the staff took over. With the paperwork completed, his wife and I left. She could not thank me enough, and when we arrived back in our town, I dropped her off and headed for home, relieved to be in one piece.

Three weeks later, Piet arrived back on the job. He showed no sign of his recent setback, and nor did he ever thank me for my help, maybe because of embarrassment; but he did treat me with much more respect after that. His effort to overcome the demons, however, did not last.

Six months later, he came into work one morning in a total state of inebriation, and broke down any door he found closed. The workers scattered when he lurched down to the factory floor, with shouts of insults and much use of bad language. The general manager called the police, who came and removed Piet from the premises. I discovered a bottle of vodka in his desk drawer and turned it in to the engineering manager, Piet's senior. This would become evidence of his disregard for company rules. The general manager fired Piet that very afternoon, and I never saw him again. To the best of my knowledge, he never completed his studies or graduated—a tragedy for one so good at his job, but who could not overcome his demons.

A month later, the general manager promoted me to head of the Work Study department, a significant step up in status and salary.

5: Never a Dull Moment

I continued on with my studies and managed to qualify as a production engineer, an achievement which gave me a small measure of status with the company. Life in the church continued on as before, but with one inclusion: I accepted an involvement with a para-church organization called The Gideons,[18] an organization of business and professional people. Adeline's boss, the owner of an electrical store and contracting company for which she did the books, happened to be the local Gideon Chairperson as well as my closest friend. The local Gideon camp met for prayer on one evening each week, plus a dinner meeting one evening per month, but my church involvement always took the higher priority. I attended all the relevant meetings every week, and did everything the pastor required of me. This commitment endured a significant adjustment after the church experienced a change in pastors, a phenomenon that occurred in the life of every fellowship from time to time.

A prominent Durban businessman and member of our denomination called the shots when changes in full-time workers became necessary. We referred to this man as "the apostle" of the movement. His business, a successful construction company, funded many of the denomination's administrative requirements, and everyone thought him to be one of the best spiritual teachers on the planet. The apostle took time off from his business to hold conventions and bring teachings to the various assemblies. I never knew what circumstances prompted the pastoral changes. Either the pastor performed poorly, or found himself in trouble with his elders, but it may also have been a way to bring different pastoral styles to bear.

I got along just fine with our church's new pastoral couple, and still did a good deal of preaching on Sunday evenings, considered as "Gospel night". My flair for evangelism, with many souls coming to know the Lord under my ministry at the time, placed me in a position of prominence and the new pastor wanted to make me an elder in the congregation, a position considered to be a great honor for any member. He introduced one caveat, however, which did not sit well with me: I had to give up my membership in the Gideon organization. For the first time in my spiritual life, I found myself at odds with the church leadership. One thing led to another, and after several hours of debate the pastor gave me an ultimatum: I could remain in the church if I refused the eldership, but would no longer be allowed to preach. My membership in a second organization, according to the pastor, detracted from my ministry as a lay-preacher and church leader. If I considered a future full-time ministry position, my membership with any other organization would not be acceptable because of divided loyalties.

I can understand this now, from their point of view; but at the time, it appeared they did not consider the Gideon movement to be a legitimate ministry, which infuriated my sense of justice. After much prayer and consideration, Adeline and I decided we could not allow the church to dictate what we did with our time. I believed that as long as I made the church my priority and attended all their meetings, I should be free to decide about involvement in other ministries, an attitude the new pastor did not find acceptable. He required my complete obedience to the call of the church ministry without any outside distractions apart from my secular job. I approached Adeline's boss, whom I shall call Edwin, a strong Christian but not a member of any church, for counsel on the matter; and he assured me that God would not condemn anyone for using their time and devotion in any aspect of His Kingdom.

After further prayer, I believed God led me to leave the church and start a bible study in my home on Sunday mornings. I told Edwin about my intentions, and he gave me his full support. He suggested we do it together, as he knew others who would definitely attend our meetings. The idea, to start another church, did not enter my mind at the time, but rather to provide a fellowship for believers who found themselves opposed to the organized church institutions. Prior to their move to our town

Edwin and his family ran a farm in an area that attracted many German immigrant farmers to our country. He and his wife, whom I shall call Lila, also involved themselves in a rural ministry run by a missionary group, an offshoot of a German religious order. The mission did good work amongst the indigenous people and became well known for miracles of healing, many which took place in their rural, evangelical meetings.

In the late 1960s, the formation of a new mission board brought in a different group of leaders who decided to change aspects of the outreach and, in so doing, alienated many of the older members. Shortly after that, Edwin and Lila endured a tragic, life-changing experience: they lost their eldest son in a traffic accident. After the death of their son, Edwin and Lila left the mission, sold up the farm, and moved to our town, where they decided to settle and buy a business. We became firm friends after Adeline got the job as their company's bookkeeper. Edwin, at least twenty years older than I, treated me like his own son, and saw in me a potential not yet realized.

Our Sunday morning bible study grew; and after several weeks, we moved the meeting out to another Gideon member's home on a farm close by. The farm also housed the local Youth For Christ[19] young person's camp, another para-church[20] organization with which I became involved through our friendship with its local leaders, Denis and Beth Drennan. The Drennans supported the new fellowship meetings and are still close friends of ours to this day.

After each Sunday morning service, several of the members stayed for lunch and played tennis on an old cement court built by the farmer. Our kids wandered down to the river to play until our tennis game ended. Everything went well for about two years, until late in 1978, when a problem arose between Edwin and his wife, Lila. Lila, a jealous woman, did not trust that a plutonic relationship existed between Edwin and his bookkeeper, (my wife Adeline). Edwin's younger brother, whom I shall call Gerry, also worked in the business; and his wife, a woman who suffered terrible arthritis to the point that it crippled her, sided with her sister-in-law. The status quo did not suit them and the relationship presented a temptation which might lead to a sinful act.

Edwin, Adeline, and I discussed the problem, and although no impropriety ever took place between them we decided for the sake of peace she should resign her position as bookkeeper and move on. Edwin promised to find her another job, but he wanted us to continue with the fellowship. Adeline and I felt the jealousy would still be present and pose a barrier to our relationships. With great reluctance Edwin agreed, but asked us to remain with the Gideon organization, as I held the position of chairman in our local camp at the time. I prayed a great deal about our spiritual future, and after a month or two decided to test the waters with regard to a return to our previous place of worship, the Assembly of True Believers. A new pastor, one who appeared to possess a more open mind now presided over the church. I paid him a visit and explained our position; as to why Adeline and I left the Assembly two years earlier. The new pastor and I bonded, and he assured me there would be no such requirements with regard to membership with para-church organizations, and I could pick up where I left off in my ministry to the church. The congregation welcomed us back with open arms.

Shortly after our return, a new evangelical vision sparked the interest of two of our four elders, and they made overtures to the pastor about the establishment of a new outreach in our town, for the solicitation of new members. The other two elders did not feel the call, and made it known that the new effort to start a "cottage-meeting" with its close proximity to the mother church, constituted a clash of mutual interest. They posited that such an outreach should be established in another town, so that members would not be pulled away from our main church body. One thing led to another, and resulted in a change of attitude among the members of the congregation. Half the church appeared to be for the outreach and the other half against. Six months later, that insidious demon of split stirred up a congregation once again.

The pastor tried in vain to pour oil on troubled waters, but several weeks later the two outreach elders, announced their desire to form a new church. I felt an extreme disappointment at their decision because the result of such an action became plain: Another nasty breakup and I decided to stay with the main body. Godfrey and Olivia, due to their move into a full-time ministry position in a small community down on the South Coast of Natal, could not be of any influence in the situation. When families left the main congregation to join the new outreach, I rallied behind the beleaguered pastor. Members, upset and confused, felt he should have had better control over the situation. The new outreach grew in membership, and after a short while numbered about fifty people, but did not yet bring in enough income to support a full-time pastor. The denomination's headquarters, situated in Durban, made many attempts to mediate between the two churches, but a wall of intolerance raged for quite an extended period of time—until the two outreach elders fell out with one another.

Members started to leave the outreach and gravitate back to the mother church. A few chose to change over to the Word of God Church, whose elders declared these orphans to have returned to the "truth." One might have wondered how these churches could endure such distractions, but many of the congregants who remained stayed out of the infighting between the polarized groups and ignored the obvious tensions. They just got on with worship and did not allow themselves to be drawn into the fray. I often thought of it as a "church within a church," where only a few knew the extent of the real problem.

*

Back at the appliance factory, my new position as manager of the Work Study department entered a new phase, where much would be demanded of my limited experience in the field of engineering.

6: An Unexpected Promotion

Our small town experienced a growth spurt due to the establishment of a large steel processing plant in the area. Over a period of three years, the sleepy hamlet expanded from its existing three thousand people to ten times the original population. Our company owned a housing project that served as accommodation for most of our factory's supervision staff and often, when new staff members with family moved into one of the houses, they made a request for an extra room or storage area to be added on to their abode. From time to time, long-term staff members also made requests for small internal changes to the layouts of their homes. The company's brick-layer, accompanied by his three-man team of helpers, made all these alterations from plans drawn up by our drawing department.

It came to pass that the company's only draftsman decided to leave town for a new job in Durban, and this enabled me to help out in the drawing department by doing the occasional house-plan alteration. I learned the basic drawing techniques from the project engineer, who did not have the time to draw up these plans himself. I also examined past drawings on file to see all the requirements for submission to the local municipality and over time became competent enough to draft plans for any domestic home or small business operation. The world economies endured some changes in the '70s due to the sudden increase in oil prices, which affected every business organization throughout the entire world. Exports of our products to foreign countries suffered, which resulted in changes to our company's labor complement. Plant economics became an even higher priority than before and resulted in the elevation of the work-study function.

The worst part of this change lay in the management's desire to cut jobs through greater labor-saving strategies, and I knew my efforts would result in workers being laid off, the price workers pay for progress, but not one I relished. The ability to implement greater overall savings to help the company's bottom line came to me with some ease and my knowledge of plant economics prospered. One day, the general manager surprised me with a visit to my office, something he rarely ever did. He walked in and placed an envelope on my desk.

"Open it. We have a surprise for you," he said.

I tore open the envelope, which revealed a letter composed on the company's official letterhead. For a brief moment, I thought my job might be in jeopardy, but the letter contained the good news of a promotion to Works Industrial Engineer. The letter outlined the reason for the appointment and my new salary structure. Not something I expected, this sudden gesture

The Bigger Picture

by the general manager overwhelmed me and it took a moment before I could respond. The general manager outlined his plan to place one of my assistants in charge of the Work Study department, which remained under my jurisdiction. My new position placed me on a team with three other engineers in charge of electrical, mechanical, and project aspects of the company. At first, I felt a fear of being under qualified for this new position; but my three comrades treated me as their equal, and it did not take long for me to fit into the new role.

Another change awaited me when the project engineer applied for a new job and moved away to Johannesburg. With the nationwide drop in foreign exports, our company's entire labor force dropped to its lowest compliment in many years. The company still ran a good profit but the management felt the need to shelve all big projects and I believed that our projects engineer saw the writing on the wall; no one spoke of a replacement and I wondered who would oversee the current projects. I soon found out their plan of action when the general manager called me into his office to inform me I would take over the project function and suggested I delegate some of my industrial engineer's work to the Work Study department. A crash course on project engineering, compliments of a book I discovered in the project's office, helped me gain a basic knowledge of the new function at hand.

Colin Setterfield

In July 1979 our main branch, situated in Durban, made a decision to close down a particular operation[21] in their home factory and move it to our town. This meant we had to plan the receipt of all the equipment and find a place for a new work area to be established; my first big challenge as the new project's engineer.

I maintained a high level of Christian witness throughout these years. Many of the factory staff avoided long conversations with me for fear that spiritual matters would arise, but I soon learned how to win them over. The need to get the shop supervisors on my side and gain cooperation for changes to the workflow in the operations under their supervision became paramount to the success of the industrial engineering function.

On the spiritual front, my return to the Assembly of True Believers Fellowship opened up new opportunities for me to lead meetings in worship and to preach on Sunday evenings. The Saturday night breaking of bread service gave further occasion for three or four lay-people to offer scriptural enlightenment to the congregation, and I made use of these times to bring words of comfort and exhortation.

Back at the factory, the establishment of the new project gained momentum and promised to keep me busy for several weeks. In order to plan out the establishment of this new venture, I often came in after-hours to spend time on the drawing board. The company ran a night shift limited to a few of the plant's major processes and the peace and quiet helped me to concentrate. As I stood at the drawing board one evening, I became absorbed by all the time constraints of the project, conscious of what actions needed to be first considerations. In the back of my mind nestled a tale which the older staff told on numerous occasions: The story featured one of the company directors who, in the earlier years, died of a heart attack in his office one day. Staff members who on occasion worked late reported that they saw the man's ghost walk down the main office corridor, a sight that threatened their future desire to come in after normal hours.

While I stood at the drawing board this one particular night, I felt the hair on the back of my neck rise significantly when a soft noise emanated from the entrance door behind me. The story of the ghost filled my mind, and with sudden fear I turned around, with my heart in my mouth. There, at the door, stood the general manager with a huge grin on his face. His sudden appearance stemmed from the need to retrieve a document from his desk drawer. When I mentioned the story of the former director's ghost, he roared with laughter and then, on a more somber note, related an experience where he, personally, saw the actual manifestation one night.

I made an instant decision that it would be better for me to come in a bit earlier in the mornings than work late in the evenings. I already spent at least four nights of the week at church and para-church meetings. Adeline always remained at home with the children on weeknights and her silent build up of resistance to my continuous attendance of every meeting escaped me. She attended church on the weekends to keep the peace with me and I, too blind at the time to heed the warning signs carried on regardless; clueless as to the real call of a father and husband. I suffered a constant need for recognition. This problem arose from an incident between my father and I a few weeks after my sixteenth birthday. I will backtrack here to explain the dynamics of this episode.

Our family's move to Durban in 1960, threw me into a litany of new experiences. A new city, a new school and a different culture exerted a substantial influence on my limited ability to adapt and my school work began to suffer due to a host of distractions. As teenagers so often do, I rebelled against the strict discipline advocated by the educational regime, and my attitude toward adult supervision caused numerous fights with my parents. One day our school principal paid my Dad a visit to let him know that my academic life teetered on the brink of disaster and unless something changed my chances of redemption appeared slim. They called me to the sitting room, and the headmaster asked where I saw myself to be in a few years. My Dad, angry and embarrassed, jumped in and said, "He's a rubbish. He'll never amount to anything in this life."

The Bigger Picture

Those words stung. After that, I began to believe my Dad might have a point; in my mind, I began to worry that my future efforts would all result in failure. The incident sparked off a determination within me to improve my performance; but in retrospect the desire to better my life stemmed from a wrong motive; I did it in an attempt to change my father's impressions of me and not for myself. After the incident my school performance improved, but despite some significant successes, the stigma attached to those cruel words could not be easily shrugged off. Perhaps my eventual gravitation toward service in the church lay in an attempt to wipe the slate clean through the establishment of a new persona, but however hard I tried, the awful stain of my dad's words remained for many years to come. It is a well-known psychological point that the same-sex parent wields the most influence in a child's life, and will determine much of that child's later behavior.

Later, my career's consequent rise from obscurity to a prominent position in a large company did eventually make an improvement to my dad's attitude, but his prior judgment of my character stayed with me for many more years—until after his death, in fact. His words that day, in the presence of the school headmaster, might have been the wakeup call I needed, but the impact on my psyche resulted in a lengthy battle with my personal self-image.

Colin Setterfield

*

At the factory, my first assignment as the company's project engineer brought a measure of excitement, plus a few scary, experiences for me. At the time, Adeline and I believed it to be God's intervention in the creation of an open door to an engineering career, and for a time my desire to be a church minister took a back seat as I threw myself headlong into the new project. Some amazing incidents lay ahead.

7: A Touch of the Miraculous

One of the fundamental aspects of Christian belief is the very personal nature of the believer's relationship with God. We believe God watches over our every step and leads us through the difficulties of life in ways that reap positive outcomes. When, however, the immediate outcome is a negative one, we fall back on the long-term prognosis of time, which will eventually bring a positive yield, be it a success or a lesson learned. This consolation is a natural reaction when one experiences interim losses despite prayer offered up for protection. After all, our entire hypothesis of God's good intention toward us rests on the fact that God is love and would never allow anything bad happen to his offspring. Therefore, negative things that happen during one's lifetime will (from a Christian believer's point of view) be attributed to either the devil's opposition or our own lack of wisdom.

Belief in a literal, personified devil responsible for all the evil in the world is another hallmark of fundamentalism—a classic case of "living in the metaphor," not the reality to which it points. We have also come to view the work of miracles, should we be fortunate enough to experience them, as a mark of God's approval on our lives. I will share some of my work experiences that could only be explained, at the time, as being miracles worked by a benevolent God, with my best interests at heart.

My new work project required me to stick my neck out in certain areas where, in order to perform some of the tasks at hand in a more confident manner, I needed more formal academic training. I expressed this concern to Cyril Thompson, the Engineering Manager and my immediate superior. He asked me to draw up a plan for the operation of the new plant, which needed to be an improvement on its previous design. I felt this to be within my existing scope of improvisation, but when the need for a new conveyor belt system became a factor, I realized I had little experience in the technical design and fabrication of such a structure. Cyril told me not to worry, that I should use standard thicknesses of the material components designed for a similar conveyor made for a past project. I pulled out the blueprints for the old conveyor and satisfied myself that I could replicate it, the only difference being the new conveyor would be a bit longer than its predecessor.

I checked all the specifications for the conveyor after the completion of the drawing, and then handed it over to Cyril for consideration. As it so happened, we both missed the implications of a crucial measurement on the actual width of this conveyor. I inadvertently used the outer measurement as an inner measurement, which made the structure several inches wider than it should have been. This mistake only came to light after the return of the completed fabrication.

It took one glance to confirm the problem. I suggested to the fabricator that their measurements lacked accuracy, but he pulled out the plan and showed us the specs for the inner and outer dimensions which confirmed the mistake to be mine. Cyril gave me the evil eye and said, "Oh great! Now we're stuck with this monstrosity. You'll have to figure out how we're going to fix this—it's far too wide. Another problem is that the conveyor belt rollers we have ordered will not fit."

I felt my face turn red. "I'm sorry, but it was an honest mistake which we both missed."

I made a suggestion. "We can weld support plates across the width to accommodate the rollers. The cost of the plates will be covered by our 15% project contingency."

Cyril stared at the conveyor for interminable seconds. "I guess that might be a quick fix. Let's go and pick up the rollers from the wholesaler."

I accompanied Cyril to the wholesaler, but on our arrival the salesperson shared some bad news.

"The factory making this type of equipment burned down last week, and we will unfortunately not receive any further supplies of the standard roller for at least six months."

Cyril Thompson frowned. "Can't we get them anywhere else? We need those rollers right now, or it will hold up the project."

The salesperson shot us an apologetic glance. "We can't source them anywhere else. I have asked several other wholesalers if they have inventory, but everyone is in the same boat."

Cyril shook his head in consternation. "We have to be up and running in three months. If we delay the supply of our product, it will result in contractual penalties."

The salesperson interjected. "I just remembered: we have had a cancelation on a bunch of rollers that are still in the warehouse. The only problem is they aren't the standard size. The purchaser has since filed for bankruptcy, and the factory said we should return them if they can't be sold."

My eyes lit up. The salesperson's suggestion sounded promising. "Exactly how wide are these rollers?" I asked.

"I'll get one and we can measure it," he said.

He returned with the oversized roller and a tape measure. I unfolded the conveyor plan on the counter, and we waited. "It's exactly 38 inches wide," he said.

I nearly fainted, but quickly regained my composure with a smile. "That is exactly the width of our conveyor. How many did you say you had?"

The Bigger Picture

The salesperson checked his records. "There are thirty-five of them."

The engineering manager gave me a knowing look. "I guess you've been talking to your old man again," he said.

I had an ear-to-ear grin on my face, because of his skepticism with regard to spiritual matters. "You have to admit that someone is looking after me," I replied.

At a later date, this story found its way into many of my sermons whenever I preached on the subject of miracles.

There is one more notable incident, which occurred about six months later. The mold on the 400-ton press[22] in the press shop suddenly cracked one day while in operation, and the run of parts could not be completed. Our company, in high production of these parts, faced severe penalties should the batch not be completed in time. When molds this large crack, there is only one fix: have a new one made. The three-week lead time for the production of such a unique piece of equipment, however, made this option impossible. Two-hundred and forty-two parts still remained after the failure of the mold, a drawback that left one us with no other choice than the employment of a specialist welder for the repair. The only problem with this choice lay in the distinct likelihood that the crack would separate again under the pressure of the press. This press stood twelve feet tall, and at least eight feet wide at the base. Everyone said the mold would give way, and a repair job a waste of our time and money.

Cyril Thompson called me in to share the problem. "We have no option but to weld this mold. Three weeks of waiting will suck every bit of profit we make on each of these items."

I shot him a quizzical glance. "I'm not sure why you're telling me this. What is it I can do?"

"You're always talking about how God looks after you. I want you to pray over that repaired mold once it's ready to go."

I couldn't believe my ears. "You're joking! You don't even believe in God," I said.

The engineering manager straightened up in his chair and smiled. "I'm ready to try anything, and we have nothing to lose. However, if it works, I will certainly be impressed."

The wind dropped out of my sails. It's one thing to acknowledge a past miracle, but to expect God to perform one to prove a point is another thing altogether and to tempt fate is never a viable practice. Unable to back out my agreement came with some reluctance.

When the morning of the target day arrived, a distinct lack of sleep complicated my early morning routine. The night, spent in solemn private prayer, included an element of the third stage of grief—much bargaining with God. I arrived at work and went straight to the press shop, where the supervisor waited with his staff. Both managers arrived, and together with the supervisor, we discussed the procedure required for me to complete the task. This would be the first time an inanimate object served as the focal point of my prayer.

The indigenous people of South Africa are a spiritual race, and most accept "Umkulinkulu" (God) as the deity everyone worshipped. They also believed in most of the biblical principles, so although our actions on that day may have appeared out of the ordinary for a work situation, it certainly did not strike them as strange. Through the witness of my faith they all knew me to be a Christian and lay preacher of a church, a position everyone respected. The Press Shop staff compliment of about fifty workers all stood in a circle around the 400-ton press and waited for me to step up to the bar. It was a huge moment for me. I placed my hands on the mold and closed my eyes. The words came with some difficulty at first, but after a few sentences, my courage began to soar. The prayer only took about twenty seconds, but when it ended, you could have heard a pin drop.

I stepped back from the press and nodded to the operator. No one moved as the system started up. I remember the intense expressions on the faces of both managers as they waited for the outcome. By agreement, the operator would press only one blank to start with, so that the mold could be inspected after the movement. The press came down with all its force, and I focused my eyes on the welded crack. When the cycle completed the operator stepped up to remove the newly formed part. My imagination played tricks on me as I scrutinized the weld. It appeared to have moved a fraction, but Cyril confirmed the repair to be good for the moment.

I nodded to the operator, and he set the press on automatic, which meant that the blanks would be fed into the mold in rapid fashion and the completed parts collected in an adjacent tray. The press did its magic, and we all watched with bated breath as part after part shot off onto the tray, perfect in every detail. Two-hundred and forty-one parts later the repaired weld opened up, and the operator turned the press off. With the first part pressed out on manual, we had the exact amount of parts required to complete the contract: a miracle in our eyes. The staff gave me a new name, "fundise", which means "wise one," a title they give to their religious ministers.

In the months that followed, my life would take another interesting turn.

8: A Change of Ownership

In 1980 the sale of our company to a British consortium brought a huge change which forced both my manager friends into an early retirement in favor of younger men from the United Kingdom. The factory underwent a complete change of corporate identity and our legal status morphed from a limited company to a corporation.

The new engineering manager, a younger man whose sole experience comprised of basic rural water systems in Kenya, saw an opportunity to bring in some of his mates from the UK. He made no bones about the fact that my job would be up for grabs as soon as he made the necessary application with the new directors. After years of a positive work experience, I now found myself on the short list to be demoted in favor of a more appropriately "qualified" person. My assistant, promoted to the position of manager of the Work Study department made it clear he would not be happy should I return to run my old department again. In our minds, it would have been a step backward for both of us. With trepidation in my heart, I made the difficult decision to leave the company in search of greener pastures.

I searched the local newspaper for work that might pay me enough to keep our home affairs running and though my job search extended to the bigger cities, we did not want to leave our town. Adeline worked at a good, secure job as a bookkeeper for the local sports shop, and we enjoyed the comforts of our modest home. It also meant a change of parish, with the time and effort required to reestablish pastoral confidences and opportunities to preach. The thought of an approach to our denomination's head office for the consideration of a pastoral position did occur, but Adeline felt such a move too risky. She made it quite clear that the ministry remained a last resort for us, and that another secular job still provided the best option.

After a short search a job that suited my qualifications came up. A large international engineering contractor with a contract to do the pipe work on a rubber manufacturing plant on the outskirts of our town required the services of a quantity surveyor. Quantity surveying represented one aspect of what I did as a project engineer, so I deemed my transferable skills to be adequate. The position offered a competitive salary with a car, a step up from my previous job. I made no bones about my strong belief in Christ when interviewed by the site manager, a young mechanical engineer from the UK and a new resident in South Africa. We bonded and became good friends. He helped me to set up a filing system and provided an overview of my duties. In those days larger companies made use of a main frame computer, for the collection of data as personal computers did not yet exist.

The Bigger Picture

After six months the main contractor's site security fired our second in command (also an engineer), for bad behavior and my boss decided not to replace the man but promoted me instead. The elevation in position increased my scope of work, plus provided a modest increase in salary, and a better car. The longer we worked on the site, however, the more concerned I became with the increased volume of welding work to be done. It seemed to me at the time that we did not have enough labor to cover the full scope of the contractual obligation. The budgeted figures based on the isometric drawings[23] of the weld requirements for the original contract did not tally with the sudden volume of work at hand, so we decided to do an in-depth study on the initial setup of the contract. It appeared that our team of consultants did not receive all the isometrics on which to base their calculations. This created an uproar between our company's top management and the main contractor in charge of all the subcontract allocations. We discovered that our company's estimators overlooked certain explanatory information about the number of duplications represented by a single iso-drawing. This oversight cost our company to the tune of millions.

As the quantity surveyor on site, part of my function entailed the establishment of all the final project costs for materials and labor, plus our calculated overheads, for presentation to the auditors. The company, bound by the original quote, faced a huge deficit and no other option remained but to absorb the loss. The final overrun turned out to be three times the contract price. Needless to say, several heads at the top rolled. The managing director charged my boss and I with the responsibility of economic frugality, to cut the losses as much as possible.

While this unfortunate state of affairs unfolded, my boss decided to take a week off. His wife, due to have their first child, requested he be available for the birth. For the first time full management of the site fell to me with the knowledge that it would be business as usual.

It turned out to be the most harrowing week of my short tenure with the company.

The Monday that followed my boss's departure started well. I arrived at work and did the regular checkups at the various work points on the site and returned to my office at about 11:00 a.m. While busy with paperwork a terse knock sounded on the door and it swung open under the hand of the site foreman, who stood on the threshold, his face a picture of despair. Behind him on the lawn stood a group of welders, the mournful expressions on their faces, a harbinger of bad news. To cope with the new estimated volume of work the company employed an extra force of 200 artisans from Portugal, and housed them all in a special camp close by. There appeared to be a problem. The foreman, with cap in hand, wiped away the tears from his eyes.

"What's up?" I asked.

The Bigger Picture

He cleared his throat. "One of the welders has just fallen off the main pipe rack and killed himself."

I stared at him in disbelief. "How?" I asked.

"He decided to move his welding shelter further along the pipe, but a gust of wind caught the shelter's fabric, and he fell twenty-five feet onto some scrap iron below. I hope you have Section 4 of the Safety Act in your office, because the site safety officer is on his way to talk to you."

I checked and found a photocopy of the safety manual on my office shelf.

The safety officer, a large Afrikaner, arrived soon after and asked to see my copy of the Act. He asked about observations that pertained to possible contraventions of protocol while on my rounds that morning. Witnesses shared their accounts of the incident and, at first, the stories all lined up—that the welder lost his footing—but none of the Portuguese welders mentioned the contravention of standard work procedure committed by the welder while up on the pipe rack. The protocol called for a welder to fold the shelter and climb down to the ground, move the shelter to the next pylon, and climb back up its ladder to access the next work point.

The testimony of what really happened came from observers busy on the furnace building adjacent to the pipe-rack. I spent five days in the site's "legal courtroom," being grilled by senior contract managers who seemed keen to find somebody to blame —and that somebody appeared to be me. I went home each night exhausted, and committed the incident to prayer. I believed God wanted me to learn something from the calamity. On the final day, when the examining body started to wrap up the conclusions, the site safety officer finally passed a verdict: that I carried no blame for the incident. Our company flew the dead welder's body back to his home country and things settled down. My boss returned from his week of leave, an excited father of a new baby girl, and thankful he had not been present when the accident occurred.

At the end of the contract, I stayed in Johannesburg at the company's head office to bring a final tally of all the costs. It took three months and I traveled 220 kilometers back and forth, between our town and the head office on weekends. The chief accountant, another Christian brother, assured me I would still have a job in the wake of the disastrous contract, but it would entail a move from my hometown to Johannesburg. A lateral movement salary-wise meant I would never be able to afford to purchase a new home due to the high prices of property in the big city.

I approached some of the industrial companies back at home to see if I might pick up work, but to no avail. The job market, at its lowest level for many years, threatened my work security and I considered that "last resort," as stipulated by my wife—a position in ministry. When I shared this with Adeline, she seemed strangely compliant on the matter, so I took the plunge and spoke to our pastor. He, in turn, spoke to the Apostle, who appeared to be acquainted with my qualifications and preaching ministry, and set up a telephonic interview. The Apostle informed me of a ministry post in a small community on the outskirts of Durban, vacated by a pastor who suffered from a stress-related illness. The Apostle arranged for me to meet with the local elders and to take their next Sunday morning meeting.

Two days later, the Apostle called to tell me the position no longer existed as the local elders favored another pastor with whom they were well-acquainted. I felt a tremendous letdown, and I think Adeline felt an equal emotion of relief. A week later the Apostle called again to say that a small fellowship on a coal mine situated about 25 kilometers outside our town, could use the services of a pastor.

"There are only eleven members, but it will help you ease into the ministry," he explained. "The two officiating elders both work on the mine, and although they have always run the meetings themselves, they feel it would be great to have a full-time worker involved."

This appeared to be a better plan for us, as Adeline could stay in her job and we didn't have to rent out our home. After my official ordination, I took my first church meeting at the mine in October 1982, and preached my first sermon as a full-time minister to the fellowship's small compliment of eleven Christians. The number of people didn't matter—I stood on the brink of a new chapter in my life. The path ahead offered a new learning experience, but a baptism into a higher form of church politics awaited me.

9: My First Commission

The congregants of the mine's assembly met in one of the utility rooms provided for social gatherings. The Sunday school compliment increased 100% with the inclusion of my three children, and a typical meeting drew eleven adults, which included Adeline and I. The two elders, always ready to accommodate, made sure we received an invitation after each Sunday morning service to a communal lunch put on by the ladies. Every Sunday my family, subjected to a morning and evening meeting with little to do but twiddle their thumbs, hated these weekend excursions. I feel so bad now as I write about this era of our lives; I appeared to be the only person to enjoy a measure of fulfillment. For the twins, ten years old, and Alison, going on thirteen, the entire religious scene constituted a nightmare. The effort to remain quiet during the services and to be on their best behavior the entire day did not sit well with them. With no other children even close to their age, it could not have been any fun in the Sunday school.

The older female members of the denomination did not dress in modern attire or use makeup of any kind, and though always neat, they exuded that drab, century-old appearance. Hair, worn either in a bun or shoulder length, remained covered under a hat or mantilla for the entire day. Not all the assemblies supported this "aged look." It depended on the elders in charge, and the older the member, the more old-fashioned the dress. The younger families pushed the envelope of modernity, despite the grumbled comments of the more legalistic members, and most of the churches enjoyed a dichotomy of styles. The head cover, however, remained a strict symbol of the woman's subservience to men. Women could not hold a pastoral or eldership position, because the executive leaders saw them as "helpers". Women could prophesy or speak in tongues, but could not stand behind a pulpit and preach.

All these rules and regulations stemmed from man's interpretation of scripture, designed to exercise control over all women; but in our day, this is what we grew up with. As an aspirant minister, I sought to be sensitive to the general church protocol, lest I be seen as a rebel and have my future ministerial path blocked by the powers that be.

I have two vivid recollections of ministry at the mine that stand out to me. I asked about the erection of a church sign, to be placed outside the building so that everyone would know about the fellowship. The lead elder, George, said it had been talked about, but no one could agree as to how the sign should look. The towns and cities erected all sorts of modern signs with lights and fancy lettering. The few old-guard congregants in the church could not identify with this secular type of billboard as being "a beacon of spirituality" for the sinner. The other elder, Corey, made a comment that the modern church signs looked more like adverts for a TV show than a marker for God's presence. I realized that any attempt to change anything in the church would be tantamount to pushing a piece of string up a steep hill. The path to any progress appeared to be littered with a gamut of personal opinions.

We decided to call a special meeting of the members after one of our Sunday morning services. I felt it necessary to discuss a few of the administrative and functional issues to see if any improvements might be made to facilitate the church's growth. After thirty minutes of deliberations, which produced no agreements on any particular change or improvement, the conversation bogged down on the matter of whether we should serve up coffee before or after the services. No one wanted to move with the times and a distinct attitude of resistance to change hung like a cloud over the gathering. I learned my lesson; no more meetings to facilitate growth or improve on existing systems.

Church elders, seen as the custodians of the assemblies they served, rested in the higher authority of their permanent appointments. A pastor contributed to the flock in the capacity of an itinerant preacher and teacher who, in time, moved on. While elders afforded their pastor every respect the long term welfare of the assembly always rested with the permanent authority. It took great patience and emotional acuity on the pastor's behalf to produce his vision in the form of palatable suggestions for the eldership to digest in a positive way.

In December of that year, about three months after I became the pastor of the mine assembly, I decided to bring a teaching on the family. To help me in setting out the two lectures required to complete the topic, I used a book obtained from our town's local Christian bookstore. The author, a well-known Christian minister and writer, provided a host of interesting principles to do with the nuclear family under God's grace. My lecture spanned two Tuesday Bible study evenings, so the two elders extended an invitation to an even smaller assembly in another mining community nearby. This assembly boasted seven members in total, but the extra bodies filled up the chairs in our hall. Despite his banishment by the Apostle to the far outreach of our spiritual vineyard the old pastor, a retired widower and known "stirrer of the pot", believed he still played a useful part in the Body of Christ.

At the first evening lecture, I told the congregation about the book used as the basis for my talks on the family, and proceeded to teach the principles. I had spoken for about fifteen minutes when the old pastor from the smaller assembly jumped to his feet and expressed his opposition to some of the content.

"It would be better if you just taught the real biblical principles straight from the Good Book rather than from this heretic's paperback!" he declared.

The Bigger Picture

This outburst took me by surprise, and I struggled to regain my composure. Our lead elder, however, came to my rescue and defended the source of my teaching. "We need to keep an open mind. The author of the book is a well-known Christian and has based his work on the scripture."

The old pastor was not to be put down. "He is also just a youngster who is caught up in New Age teachings. I believe his message is from the devil!"

A few of the others weighed in on the conversation and hijacked the evening's topic away from the intended study of the nuclear family. The conversation became directed toward the younger people of the day, whom the stalwarts felt dispensed with the tried, biblically-based traditions of the church in favor of heretical teaching. They posited that church sermons contained too much psychology, and some of the folk saw this as a bad influence on people. It conflicted with the message of the Cross, they said. I attempted to bring the subject back on course, but the people seemed more intent on arguing the pros and cons of changing values. In the end, I abandoned the talk on the family and ended the meeting. The old pastor and his six members left without saying goodbye, and we all breathed a sigh of relief. I knew they would not be back for the second lecture, nor did I care. The old "brother" would call the Apostle, no doubt to tell him that the denomination should get rid of the heretic in charge of the mine assembly, and make sure that the book on the nuclear family was banned from use in our group. The lead elder, George, assured me that the Apostle knew the old pastor's penchant for trouble wherever he went, and that the story would be taken with a pinch of salt.

I endured four more months of travel back and forth to the mine from our hometown; the realization soon dawned that my wife and three children gained no enjoyment from the church meetings and with the assembly showing no sign of growth under my ministry, doubts about God's call on my life clamped down on my faith like a vice. After six months, however, the family settled down in acceptance of the status quo and we soldiered on.

In early March 1983, I received a call from the Apostle to inform me of a pastoral move which left a vacancy in a small KwaZulu-Natal[24] town of about two thousand people. He wanted me to move into this parish and start ministering within two weeks. The two elders charged with its oversight both ran successful businesses; one owned the local grocery store and the other a hardware shop. The church boasted thirty registered members with a church building and a manse situated on an acre of ground. I had an interview with the two elders, both good men who loved the Lord and supported mission work among the indigenous people. The local primary school provided education for children up to standard five (grade seven) with older children in attendance of a high school in another community some fifty kilometers distant.

Adeline and I discussed the virtues of sending our daughter, now a teenager, to this high school, but the curriculum did not offer piano tuition. We really wanted her to continue with music so I made the choice that she take up board and lodging with our ex-neighbors in the old home town. After two weeks, however, this arrangement did not work for her, and we found another home with friends of ours, also members of the Assembly of True Believers church. More thought should have been invested in this decision as we soon discovered that these arrangements did not serve the best interests of my daughter. In an act of selfishness, I forged ahead confident in the misguided philosophy, that God would take care of all the details.

After six months my daughter told us she wanted to come home despite the loss of music as a prime subject. After some diligent research Adeline and I discovered we could get her into a prestigious boarding school at Pietermaritzburg, with a curriculum that offered all her current subjects, but Alison no longer wanted to be separated from her family. She concluded that the boarding school the twins attended would suffice for her but both Adeline and I felt she should not drop her music, a decision I now deeply regret. It is my understanding that those years of separation from us caused a deep resentment of my position as a father and protector.

Our new sleepy hollow, however, turned out to be one of the best experiences of my ministerial career. The sugarcane fields, green and beautiful, extended as far as the eye could see; the town, close-knit and friendly, offered a relaxed atmosphere plus a squash court, the one sport I enjoyed. Not far from our town the legislative capital of KwaZulu-Natal, Ulundi, provided good construction opportunities for small business and the head of the Inkatha Freedom Party, Chief Mangosuthu Buthelezi, presided over the homeland parliament, under King Goodwill Zwelithini.

Many rich experiences awaited me as a pastor in this homely place, and I soon found I could continue doing architectural drawings, which supplemented my minister's stipend. Adeline managed to get a job as secretary to the regional professional engineer, who became my close friend and squash associate. Graham also presided over the local Anglican church, so we had our faith in common.

I will never forget the first night I slept in the old manse. It became a standing joke for many years to come.

10: Sorry, My Mistake

The old farmhouse manse, or the "Rat House" as we referred to it, stood on an acre of ground across the road from the church hall. The Assembly owned both plots of ground, a testament to the faithfulness of the eldership and the financial support their businesses offered. I moved in alone, mid-month in March 1983, while Adeline worked out her two weeks' notice at the sports shop in our hometown. Arrangements had been made to rent out our house, and Alison would move in with our neighbors across the road. I planned to travel back, a distance of about 110 kilometers each way, to bring her home for the weekends.

My poor daughter; so miserable without her family and I, too caught up in my ministry to notice the effect on her, lived on in my world of fundamental religiosity. I believed in those days that God made a way for everyone to be happy, but not without a certain amount of sacrifice. My short-sightedness and naivety with regard to God's dealings with his children led to a rift between Alison and I which lay close beneath the surface of our relationship for many years to come. What I thought to be faith became a subtle form of presumption.

Colin Setterfield

On my arrival at the manse, a quick look around the furnished home resulted in a few concerns. The one-hundred year-old farm abode, built on the original land before the establishment of the town, looked more like a fortress than a dwelling. It had four bedrooms, a large dining room in the center of the building, and one room that served as a thoroughfare to a large bathroom with toilet and shower. The addition of an office with its own outside door served as my plan-drawing room for the extent of our stay. I soon learned that the house harbored a multitude of rats, who entered in under the footings from outside and used the gap between the hardwood floor and its concrete base as their command center. They also migrated into the roof, where their fecal signs could be seen on the topside of the ceilings.

I discovered a tiny hole in one of the corridors where the critters gained access into the house's interior and did my best to block it up, but the little devils chewed through almost anything I placed over the hole. Finally, I resorted to a metal cover. It would not be uncommon, though, for us to see one of the creatures scurry down the hallway and disappear into a new hole somewhere else in the house. Little wonder the twins called it the Rat House. Our long-legged English Fox Terrier, Tag, on regular patrol duty, deposited the carcasses in the kitchen to the utter consternation of our house maid.

The Bigger Picture

On that first night, everything seemed so different and strange. The small town died completely after six pm, and the black people who worked in local businesses headed back to their homes in Ulundi. The branches of several tall trees on the side of the house often scraped against the gutter when the wind blew from a certain direction, and the leaves of six large avocado trees in the backyard, rustled in any moderate breeze. A wooden structure which appeared to be a storage shed occupied one back corner of the lot, but I soon discovered that it served another purpose altogether.

Earlier on in the evening I did not see a vehicle parked in the shadows of an avocado tree adjacent to the driveway but at about 11:30 pm the noise of closing car doors and an attempt to start the engine awoke me from my sleep. I jumped out of bed, pulled the bedroom curtain aside to check on my car parked in the doorless garage, separate from the house, but could not see anything in the darkness. It is common in South Africa for most people to keep a revolver close at hand for personal protection and in the heat of the moment I feared for the safety of my vehicle. I picked up the .357 Magnum, a birthday gift from Adeline, and crept out to the back verandah, which faced the garages and outhouses. Halfway down the driveway I saw an SUV with a group of men in quiet conversation with each other; the whole scene appeared strange to me so I raced out into night with my revolver in hand.

"Stop right there!" I shouted. "What are you trying to do?"

The four men stared in horror at the gun in my hand.

"Don't shoot, Boss. We are from the church."

I kept the gun trained on them. "But why are you trying to steal this vehicle?"

"We are not stealing it, Boss. It's Boss Stan's vehicle. We use it to pick up the committee members and we use the shed in the back of the yard for our meetings."

I felt sheepish. "I apologize. I'm the new pastor of the assembly, and I arrived this afternoon. I wasn't told about the meetings in the shed. I thought someone was trying to steal my car out of the garage."

We all had a good laugh, and after further introductions, they left. The next day, I visited Stan at his store and related the story, but he already knew about the incident. "Perhaps it's better to trust in the Lord than the gun," he said.

Two weeks later, the rest of my family arrived and we settled into the new home. Our big German Shepherd soon discovered that many people walked up and down our road to the town center, and he delighted in mock attacks which stopped short at the fence between the yard and the street. It didn't take long for the victims to find a different route to their various destinations.

The Bigger Picture

Our first church meeting as a family drew all the members, and the small hall filled up to capacity; thirty-seven worshippers in total. A communal lunch took place afterward, and we felt like the proverbial goldfish in a bowl. The twins, Paul and Andrew, soon made friends and acquainted themselves with all the places where they could spend time getting up to mischief, as young boys do. Alison, on the other hand, did not share our spirit of excitement. The small community offered few teenage prospects with whom she could make friends, but after several weeks she formed a relationship with Stan's second oldest son, Chris, aged sixteen years. Nothing could ever come of the relationship, however, because of her school and board arrangements.

The twins, aged eleven, entered grade six in the local primary school and loved every aspect of the friendly, laid-back atmosphere of the town. They scouted out areas where they could ride their BMX bicycles, and we seldom saw them at all during the day. Released from the oppressive Sunday travel and somber meetings of the mine assembly, they began to enjoy their after-school and weekend playtimes.

I joined the local squash team for recreative activity and became good friends with Graham, the area's professional engineer and Anglican minister (our number one player), Barry the local butcher (the team's number two) and Dave, a young single man who worked construction in Ulundi. In the playoffs, for team positions, I managed to take the number three spot, which left Dave in fourth. This period constituted the best three years of my squash career.

In the second year, our squash team received some very sad news one morning: Dave, our number four player, died as the result of an unfortunate accident the previous night while traveling back to the town from Ulundi after work. After a double shift he fell asleep at the wheel and his car veered off the road to be impaled by the fender-high steel barrier, which caught the vehicle front center. The barrier tore right through from front to back, and virtually sliced him in half. The road from Ulundi saw very few cars late at night, and sadly the wreck sat impaled on the barrier for two hours before someone came across it. Our little enclave did not have a medical clinic, so the people who found him rushed through to the hospital in the next town, thirty kilometers away. The young man hung onto life by a thread, but in the end lost too much blood and he passed away on the operating table.

We also enjoyed some amusing experiences during that time, things that only happen to ministers. I visited my congregation at least twice every month, and often took Adeline with me. One afternoon we visited a lady I shall call Harriet. Harriet, in her late eighties, suffered some dementia and stayed with her equally aged husband. We wanted to introduce ourselves, as they no longer attended the church meetings but still considered themselves members. I knocked on the door and waited. After a few more hard knocks, I heard a shuffle, and the door flew open to reveal Harriet in nothing more than a diaper. She greeted us and asked who we were. At that moment, the old man dressed in his underpants, wandered down the passageway and stopped in the entrance hall behind his wife.

Harriet stared at us with glassy eyes. "I'm going to take my nap now, come back later," she said.

We both felt like courtroom exhibits as the old man's eyes raked us from head to toe and as Harriet turned around, her diaper fell off to reveal a shriveled up old backside, framed between two bony hips. Adeline just looked at me as I closed the door and we held our laughter until the end of the driveway, where we could contain it no longer. I felt bad about our mirth over the incident, because these two old people needed help and should have been placed in palliative care. The image of that wrinkled old backside still lingers in my memory. I reported the incident to Stan, who called some family members in Durban. The next week a woman arrived and transported the old couple to an old-age home, where I'm sure they received the treatment they deserved.

Another time, we visited an old-age home in the town down the road to do some outreach ministry. I took my guitar, and some of the folks from our church came along to support the meeting. A group of people in their late eighties sat around in a circle, about fifteen people in all, and I played a few well-known worship songs. Everyone chimed in with gusto, and after the last song, I made ready to bring a short word of encouragement. I opened my Bible and started to read a verse of scripture when one of the old ladies, in an armchair with a blanket over her legs, jumped up. The blanket fell off onto the floor and revealed the naked bottom half of her body.

"I have to go and play tennis now," she said.

It took me a while to regain my composure. After that, I wanted to escape, lest anyone else needed to play any sport.

In 1984, Alison moved to the boarding school in Pietermaritzburg, where she started grade eight. The roundtrip, at least five hundred and fifty kilometers, took a full day's travel and a full tank of gas. Meanwhile the twins moved to the boarding school in the town down the road, but were able to come home every weekend.

Despite some of these drawbacks, Adeline and I carry fond memories of our sleepy-hollow fellowship and the time we spent there. After a period of almost three years a new call, however, would be made on our ministry.

11: A Brief Interlude

The reader may wonder at this point what purpose all these experiences serve in a book that deals with a shift in belief systems. But foundations and backgrounds are always important to any life story, despite controversial conclusions. We all live our lives in the midst of controversy. Questions about origins, endings, and our status in this Universe abound. Every bit of knowledge gained, every experience good or bad, helps to shape our belief system and guide it toward an eventual understanding of our own reality. All questions with regard to an infinite Creator that may emanate from our different philosophies still require the element of faith to draw final conclusions. It's not that I can lead anyone to a deity in material form and say "this is God;" and as much as we may be convinced of the Creator's presence, proof remains very much a matter of faith. Our need to discuss the realm of the spirit made it necessary to develop words for concepts that are not of a material or physical nature.

Causality (cause and effect) is the only real smoking gun that can lead us to believe in a Creator. An effect arises from a cause: because the world exists, something must have caused it. Human nature does not live easily with mysteries, so we lean on our faith to solve the dilemma. Our faith indicates that the most obvious reason for the existence of our universe is a Creator. Most humans will spend the rest of their lives in an effort to prove or disprove this concept; but for many, the notion appears to have been hardwired into their thoughts.

The real question, for me, is not the existence of the Creator but rather how the Creator deals with creation. All ancient religions portray a host of similar revelations about our reality. They all contain a measure of myth, historical truth, and the experiences of devout people who lived in an age long ago. It is such a great pity that human nature chooses to find one piece of a puzzle and live as though that were the whole picture!

The reason why I relate many personal ministerial experiences as a backdrop to the paradigm shift in my belief system is to provide the reader with an overview of human actions and reactions to the application of faith, and why I personally came to an understanding of the bigger picture. Almost four decades of church involvement, from the pew to the pulpit, has afforded me the privilege of making in-depth assessments about what actually works and what is just human perception.

So far, I have attempted to portray how fundamental believers fail to be objective about differences of opinion and live in peace with other chosen points of view. The inevitable split is the way most doctrinal arguments are sorted out, and in many of these breaks in fellowship, it is rare for offended parties to get over the problem. In my opinion, the reason for many of these schisms is that we take opposition to our pet theories too personally. It is, perhaps, a human trait that we build our personal self-worth upon our chosen belief system. When someone contradicts our belief, it is viewed as an attack on our character—that we are stupid to believe whatever it is we accept as a truth.

A change in my personal perception, however, came about through the realization that each person sees things in their own unique way. Not one of us can claim expertise in spiritual truth because we "see through a glass darkly," and our reality is formed through the eye of faith and imagination. Although we use scripture as the foundation for our belief, we need to understand a reality about Verse, 2 Timothy 3:16, upon which the supposed inerrancy of scripture is founded: "...all scripture is given by inspiration of God...". The word inspiration does not mean word-for-word dictation. The Greek word for inspiration is "God-breathed," which means the Creator transferred life principles to the human mind as though they were "breathed" into our consciousness. Here, we again see the metaphoric application (of breath) necessary to provide the human mind with an answer with regard to a transfer of information that will identify with human concepts. This gave the writers of scripture the need to inject many humanisms into its fabric in order to make the stories more digestible and knowable.

It is the main reason why we have inclusions of gender, heaven and hell as destinations, a "kingdom" as the overall concept of God's domain, the rulership of a king, the nuclear family as the structure of relationships, and many more such figures of speech. Another problem is that a serious study of the history of ancient scripture will reveal the sketchiness and often lack of reality in many cases that surround biblical events as recorded, in most cases long after the fact. It is therefore not feasible to say that the scriptures are without error or infallible, because humans are fallible.

The change I experienced over the time of my Christian walk does not rest in any one aspect of scriptural ambiguity, but more on how we as Christians live out the truths we believe in. Our understanding is often obscured by the inconsistencies we have learned to live with; incongruities that should alert us to some of the unrealistic conformities imposed by a fundamentalist religious lifestyle. The average believer does not try to think all these things through, but if a minister hopes to teach others the right way, it is necessary to place everything under a microscope.

I have often wondered why people slip into the fundamental rut with such ease, when there is so much proof of a bigger picture around us. When I analyze what I perceived to be my truth, it became clear (to me) that the Creator did not hide spiritual realities, but placed them in plain sight. I want to reassert that there is nothing wrong with a fundamental, conservative belief as long as its application doesn't hurt, denounce, or exclude others from living their lives in their chosen way. Over the time of my church involvement, at a working level in the Faith, I look back now and understand where my misconception of reality stemmed from. Well-meaning zealots taught us that all souls not "born again" end up in hell. In the fundamentalist camp, being born again is huge. It is the gateway to salvation, and the only way a human being may have a relationship with God. It is common Christian practice that the believer should love the sinner and pray for the deliverance of their souls, but to be good Christians we need to be separate from them, for what fellowship does darkness have with light? I am a child of the light, and the unbelievers are the children of darkness. I am on my way to heaven, and they to a Christ-less eternity. I see now that deep down, and without realization, a superiority complex developed within my own thinking. God chose me over them, and therefore I am a better person. This is a very subtle reflection of the human ego.

*

Living in the Metaphor: 25

As good, practicing Christians, we instruct ourselves to ignore the ego's demands for recognition as superior beings, in favor of more humble platitudes. We think that complete transformation comes via "a change of heart" through verbal utterances, words that invoke a salvation not shared with the rest of the world. If we rest only in the words, however, we fool ourselves. To become a new creature in Christ is far beyond mere lip service. The sinner's prayer and the acceptance of a savior into one's heart is a highly metaphoric inculcation of real principles that should lead to a complete change in outlook and behavior. If we remain in the metaphor and fail to embrace it as a bridge to reality, we will not change in real terms.

We may have succeeded in the performance of a church ritual and thereby appeased those around us who are witnesses, but we will remain in a small box of metaphoric fundamental clichés. To be born again is not merely a practice reserved for those who adhere to Christian teachings, but to all people who long for eternal truth. The metaphor will challenge us to seek the reality, and that reality is far more tangible than we ever anticipated; reality goes beyond the concept of a mere group of people who believe a certain way. It touches the hearts of all humanity, and embraces everything in the entire universe. The born again experience, in terms of reality, is the conscious decision to conform to the love of the one infinite creator. It is a shift in our

The Bigger Picture

consciousness from the dualistic concept of "God and I" as distinct separate entities to "one and the same".

Fundamentalists have highjacked the word "saved" and transformed it into a special status, a necessary transition that gains the complete acceptance of God. The true meaning of 'being saved' is now lost to those who do not follow the Christian faith. The bigger picture truth of reality with regard to salvation goes far beyond religious borders, because it relates in real terms to every human being. To be saved, in terms of reality, is to come to the realization that you as a human being are connected to everything in the universe, and that your mind is not separate from the mind of the Creator. Salvation is not a step you take to gain acceptance or a free pass into heaven (although this is how metaphors may seem to work in scripture).

A metaphor is a picture that points to a reality but is not in itself that reality. The reality of salvation is the peace you gain with regard to your personal standing (along with everyone else) in the eyes of the Creator, a standing you have always had and can never lose. It is a picture of the Creator who enjoys the wonders of creation and life through you, a vessel chosen before time began.

One of the factors that led to my later transformation came from a study of spiritual-population demographics. Approximately 7.2 billion people lived on the planet in 2012. Without going into too much detail, the statistics at the time showed that although one-third of the total number considered themselves to be Christians (about 2.3 billion people) a smaller percentage of this "third" believe in a conservative, fundamental evangelical Christianity with a strict belief in literal translation and inerrancy of scripture. If I considered the numbers (based on the above), it would mean that a huge number of human beings (out of 7.2 billion) would be considered as lost. I wondered if a loving God would subject so many people to a place of hellfire and damnation.

All ancient scripture in the world's religions make great use of metaphoric figures of speech to reveal the truths of reality. They are rich in symbolism and poetic narrative, and the reason for this is that matters of the spirit are beyond the comprehension of human faculty. In order to gain some understanding of spiritual values, we have developed a language which is highly metaphoric. The point I would like to make here is that in the use of the metaphor, the fundamentalist inclination is to stick with the metaphor and ignore the reality it is supposed to reveal. We decide to live in the metaphor and not the reality it points to. Fundamentalists of all religions will take a huge step toward the bigger picture if they realize this one fact: the metaphor is there to guide them into reality, not cut them off from it. The reality is to be taken literally, not the metaphor. Unfortunately, many see reality to be a work of the devil, who wishes to pull the wool over our eyes and deceive us. We come to believe through wrong

The Bigger Picture

teaching that reality is evil, and we will end up in hell if we make reality our final point of view. The events will, however, help us to interpret the reality contained in the metaphor.

Now: Let us return to our sleepy-hollow fellowship in Kwa-Zulu-Natal.

12: A New Horizon

Life in our new fellowship could not have been better. Everyone seemed happy with my ministry, and I found fulfillment at every level. The architectural drawing business took off due to the expansions in Ulundi, the KwaZulu-Natal Capital, and provided me with as much work as I could handle. The church subsidized our rent and paid all the utilities, so monthly expenses remained minimal. We often received regular gifts in the form of groceries, or envelopes, (left in our letterbox) which contained money. A further opportunity arose when the local municipal building inspector retired from his job due to ill health and Graham, the local professional engineer, approached me to take over the building inspections on houses being built in the two main suburbs of our town.

Not only did I get to do all the building inspections, but the municipality also contracted me to scrutinize the building plans before they were passed on to Graham for a final check-over. Adeline worked half-days, five days per week, which left the afternoons free for her artwork. Although we were very happy, our poor daughter, Alison, missed her family and hated the school hostel accommodation. She wanted to be home with us, but there seemed no alternative at the time. I made the trip to Pietermaritzburg twice a month to pick her up at midday on a Friday, then drove straight back to our town. We would leave again early Monday morning to get her back to school by 8:00 a.m.

One day in July 1985, I received a phone call from an old friend whom I will call Derek. We worked together in earlier years while I managed an oil depot and he visited once every six weeks to audit my work. Over the period of my tenure there we became good friends and I shared many aspects of my faith with him. His call served to inform me that he had left his job to go into the Christian Ministry as a pastor of a small church in a growing community, situated in the province of the Eastern Transvaal, now known as Mpumalanga. Their fellowship, which I shall call the Eternal Life Church, grew at a rapid rate, and he needed to appoint an assistant pastor to help with all the meetings. Pastor Derek spoke of a "vision" given him by God one day while in prayer; the city in which they lived would be open for evangelism, and he (Pastor Derek) would be God's chosen instrument to build a megachurch with a Christian school. Pastor Derek shared that their church services sustained an extensive move of the spirit and that the people loved the freedom this style facilitated. This group of churches believed in a prosperity doctrine, where the pastor established the work from grassroots and directed all operations. Elders did not hold secular jobs, but became full-time pastors in the work.

Pastor Derek wanted to know if I might consider a position as an assistant pastor in the work. The offer took me by surprise, and I said I would pray about it. Our lives seemed so idyllic and peaceful in our sleepy hollow that it caused me not to take his offer seriously until a reality check made me think of the future. Our town's limited size offered the church little prospect of future growth. In accordance with the denomination's general model, the Apostle would eventually move me somewhere else, and our fortunes could change dramatically overnight. I entertained the possibility that God might be calling me to a new field of service.

Pastor Derek invited us over for a weekend to experience the dynamics of their fellowship so I made arrangements with Stan to take the Sunday meetings. I did not tell him about the offer, but said I needed a little time off.

The Eastern Transvaal terrain appeared bleak in comparison with Natal's more tropical vegetation, and the area sported several large electric power generating plants. Opencast coal mines dotted the landscape, a vista which evoked negative first impressions as we drove through the regional district toward the city. It concerned me that Adeline might not approve of our potential new home.

The Bigger Picture

Pastor Derek's church surprised me in its size and dynamics. The Eternal Life Church boasted a recent surge in membership and a total of about three hundred people broke bread every Sunday morning. A new church building, still under construction, accommodated everyone in a single hall that could hold about one thousand souls. An elaborate double door entrance opened up into a large reception area conjoined by three offices, toilets, a small chapel, a large kitchen and utility room, which all catered to the staff and congregational needs. At one end of the open area a set of double doors led into the main assembly hall.

We attended a Friday-evening gathering for the church's home group leaders at which Pastor Derek officiated. The people came across as friendly, respectful and enthusiastic about the Lord's work. Adeline and I enjoyed the music, which seemed more alive and modern in comparison with the choruses we sang in our home assembly. One particular tune stuck in my head and, a few days later, back at home, I tuned into a Christian radio program to hear the same tune heard in the meeting at Eternal Life Church. I prayed much about the pros and cons of such a move, and I began to look for a sign—anything that might help me make the decision. It so happened I needed to travel to Durban for a denominational church convention the next day, so I left early in the morning. The potential move rested heavily on my mind as I traveled down through the mountainous terrain to pass through the town where the boys attended boarding school.

As I came over the crest of a hill, a large removal van parked on the side of the road caught my eye. My jaw dropped when I saw the name of the moving company painted on the van's side. The name of the outfit, preceded by the location of the city's head office turned out to be the city where Pastor Derek ran his ministry.

A sign from God. I took it as God's direct word to me about the move, and I made up my mind we would take Pastor Derek up on his offer. When I returned from the convention that night, I told Adeline about the experience. She felt conflicted about the move, but our daughter, Alison, about to enter her final year of school received the news with enthusiasm as the new city's co-ed high school offered music as a subject. Eventually, Adeline agreed the move would open up new avenues for us, so I contacted Pastor Derek to let him know we would move at the end of November 1985. I broke the news of our decision to Stan, and he confessed that the Apostle had already spoken to him about a possible move for me. A larger assembly in Durban required the services of a new full-time worker; he felt it would fit my profile. With a measure of trepidation I called the Apostle to inform him I would be heading for new horizons. The expected rebuke never came and he surprised me with a good report on my ministry, plus a well-wish for my future. In the ardent belief that the new opportunity proved God's good intentions toward me I set my sights on the new position at the Eternal Life Church.

The Bigger Picture

Our new church rented a comfortable home for us to move into and Stan offered his truck, plus a crew of three helpers, to move all our goods and chattels to the new city. Alison said goodbye to boarding school life, and we settled down in our new habitat. I didn't realize at the time that the change would bring some extreme situations into my life; changes that would elevate me to new heights of ministry... but at a cost.

13: A Mandate for Children's Education

Pastor Derek eased me into a visitation program that allowed me to get to know the members of the congregation. I also took a few Sunday evening meetings, did hospital visitation, and got involved with the building expansion program. Pastor Derek knew of my architectural ability, hence my first commission: to draw up and finalize plans for a daycare center; we then found a contractor to start the building under my supervision. We worked hard, doing much of the grunt-work ourselves in order to save costs; a contractor put up the brick walls and installed the roofing.

Pastor Derek employed a full-time daycare supervisor and once the facility passed muster many of the church members transferred their children from other centers in the city. We gained new church members through this, and the fellowship grew steadily over the next year to about six hundred people. Income from tithes and offerings reached new heights, which allowed us to start the next phase of growth: a Christian school. I drew up the plans for this project and sent them into the local municipal authorities. Our contractor started the project in July 1986 and completed the construction by the end of the year.

The Bigger Picture

Pastor Derek's research on the latest initiative called the Accelerated Christian Education system led to our adoption of the method designed for use in Christian schools around the world. These schools used a system of "pacers," books that facilitated self-learning and employed one teacher to preside over as many as one hundred students with the help of class monitors. The monitors did not have to be qualified teacher's assistants, but needed to have passed a matriculation level of education in order to help the young students with difficulties experienced in the learning process. The single, qualified teacher allocated to each learning center would deal with the more difficult concepts when required. It would be common to have as many as five classroom monitors under one teacher in a large learning center. The teachers and monitors all attended several weeks of tuition on the system before the school opened in the following year.

Pastor Derek appointed me as the headmaster of the school, a job I would perform in conjunction with my pastoral duties, and in January 1987 we opened the doors to about sixty students, all the offspring of our local church members. The school fees helped pay for the teachers and monitors plus all the classroom desks, chairs, and relevant furniture. My life and ministry rode the crest of a euphoric wave until halfway through the second year of the school's existence when Pastor Derek responded to an offer by a pastor who ran a large independent ministry in the United States. The American pastor offered accommodation to ministers from developing countries for a one month educational visit to his facility on a farm close to one of the big American cities. The idea behind the invitation: to teach interested ministers from churches around the world how to build up and run a large mission organization. The pastor's claim to fame lay in his very successful operation which included a large church congregation, a Christian school, and a university, all facets of ministry that interested Pastor Derek.

In Pastor Derek's absence I took charge of our church and school, a huge responsibility for me, but I embraced it with my usual sense of commitment. A few weeks prior to Pastor Derek's departure Adeline and I purchased our first home in the city, a work in progress which the previous owner, a contractor, could not complete due to time constraints before his move to another city. Perched on a hill, the house offered us a magnificent view of the entire area, but many things needed to brought to completion, such as the main bathroom wall tiles and dining room floor. An en suite bathroom, and some roof tiles also required completion, all work I could do on my own time. The church meetings and operation of the ministry, however, came first, which left little time for this construction; but I worked at it in stages.

One Saturday morning, while involved with some repairs on our new home's roof, one of the deacons dropped in to see me.

The Bigger Picture

"You are needed at the hospital, Pastor Colin!" he declared. "A church member's husband has been involved in a motor accident, and she has asked that you come down to Emergency."

I climbed down off the roof, washed my hands, and pulled on a jacket. "Who is the member?" I asked.

"The wife is not really a member, but has come to our church several times, and she asked for you specifically," responded the deacon. "Her husband's name is Peter Robinson."

I shot over to the hospital and walked into the Emergency Room, where I found an elderly woman with two children in the waiting room. "I'm looking for Mrs. Robinson. I'm the assistant pastor at the Eternal Life Church," I told the woman.

She wiped a tear from her eye. "They're in a side room, adjacent to the operating theatre down the passage, to your left. The news is not good, I am afraid."

I thanked her and walked down the hallway until I found the room. A woman with ginger-colored hair sat on a chair next to the bed, upon which lay the body of a man covered with a sheet. Only his head could be seen, and I noticed a distinct disfigurement of his forehead. "I came as soon as I heard the news," I said.

She looked at me with sad, tear-filled eyes. "There was nothing they could do for him. The brain damage was too severe."

"How did it happen?" I asked.

"It happened outside the city, near one of the power stations. Ironically, Peter had slowed down because of an accident that had taken place moments before, and I guess he wanted to see what happened. A large truck approaching at speed from behind could not stop in time, and crashed into the back of Peter's van, crushing it almost beyond recognition. The other man in the front seat next to him was killed instantly, but Peter survived and was brought here, where he passed away on the operating table about ten minutes ago."

I had never been that close to a corpse before, and for a moment it unnerved me. Mrs. Robinson and I prayed together while I tried to gather my wits as to what to do next.

"Is there someone who can help you with the funeral arrangements?" I asked.

"My mother and father will help. We have called Peter's brother; he will stay with us until everything is finalized. I'm worried about the children, though."

"I will speak to them," I said.

We moved out to the waiting room, where the woman's mother and the two children waited. Few people will know what it is like to inform family members of the death of their loved one. In these situations, there aren't words that suffice, and it is best to say as little as possible. In my previous church, the sleepy hollow fellowship, only one death occurred during my tenure there: the alcoholic husband of one of our older members drank himself to death while on a fishing trip.

As we entered the waiting room, the two children, a boy of twelve years and a girl of ten, ran to their mother and they embraced each other. Both children eyed me with apprehension as I sat them down next to me to share the bad news.

The boy turned back to his mother and, in a trembling voice, shared an experience both children swore they witnessed moments before we joined them. "We have just seen Granny and Grandpa walk right past us and continue along the hallway toward the reception. When we called out to them, they ignored us."

Mrs. Robinson senior shrugged her shoulders. "I didn't see anybody. I don't know what the children are talking about."

Both children were emphatic they had seen their grandparents. When I enquired of Mrs. Robinson about the grandparents, she said, "Peter's parents have been dead for several years."

Then I understood, and turned to the children. "They must have come to escort your dad to Heaven."

Four days later I took the funeral. I visited Mrs. Robinson and her two children a few times after that, but she never returned to the church again.

The church meetings progressed well in Pastor Derek's absence. One Sunday evening, I preached a sermon on revival that solicited a huge response from the congregation. The next day I visited Pastor Derek's mother-in-law, charged with the care of her grandchildren in the pastoral couple's absence. I checked up on them every week to make sure the kids behaved. Pastor Derek's mother-in-law greeted me at the door with a huge smile.

"I just want to thank you for the wonderful meeting we had yesterday," she said. "Derek called late last night to speak to the children and I mentioned it to him—that we have never experienced such a move of the Spirit."

The moment she spoke the words, I sensed a check in my own spirit, concerned at how Pastor Derek might construe the news. Although no jealousy problems evidenced themselves in our relationship my experience confirmed that more congregants gravitated toward me for counsel when required. I detected that the people found my pastoral ministry more sympathetic than Pastor Derek's. He also lacked popularity with the more business-minded members, who wanted a very thorough report every month on the financial details of the ministry. Pastor Derek always played the cards close to his chest, and though I believe he never did anything dishonest with the money, he could have been more forthcoming. I know he sensed the mood of the people, due to a swing in whom they chose to go to for counsel, but the matter never came up in our conversations.

The Bigger Picture

Nevertheless, the distinct notion of a significant shift in the spirit world, invaded my peace. This became evident when Pastor Derek and Elaine returned to South Africa. I travelled to the airport to meet them and detected a distinct change of attitude on our mutual greeting of one another. On the drive home, they were both very reserved. Apart from a few questions about the children I experienced a disconnect with regard to the welfare of the church. I asked how they enjoyed their stay in the USA, and received one-word answers.

"We'll talk about it later. We just want to get home and see the kids again," said Pastor Derek.

I dropped them off at their home and received no invited to stay, something I thought unusual, as they did not seem all that tired.

The next morning when I arrived at the church, Pastor Derek called me into his office. I thought he might apologize for their coldness on the trip back from the airport—an incorrect assumption on my behalf.

Colin Setterfield

14: A Sticky Situation

What I feared has come upon me... Job 3:25

Perhaps there's much to be said about the above quote from the book of Job. Adversity stalks every one of us; the popular notion with respect to personal calamity is that because we feared it in the first place, it pursued us. I wouldn't, however, be too quick to lay the cause of adversity at the feet of self-inflicted fear. Should this sentiment have been a hard-and-fast rule, the first air flight I ever took, at the age of six years, would have resulted in a crash—which it didn't. There may be some truth that fear perverts our sense of discernment when we are confronted with a calamity, but the fact that I entertain fear does not necessarily attract the calamity to me. What does bring us into the court of adversity, however, are the decisions we make in that confrontation.

I doubt I ever feared a breakdown in my relationship with Pastor Derek. We had always kept up a positive dialogue about ministry and a respect for one another's position in the eyes of the people so they would have confidence in our leadership. I felt Pastor Derek saw my participation in the work as valuable and necessary for the growth of the ministry under his oversight. That a valid reason might exist as to why he would suddenly want me out, never occurred to me but in the absence of any concrete evidence of wrongdoing on my behalf, I started to imagine possibilities of misperception on his behalf. Might he have become jealous that the people appeared to gravitate toward me? Did fear of a shift in popularity cause him to see me in a different light?

I can honestly say I never contemplated a takeover over of the church under such conditions. Pastor Derek sometimes spoke about his desire to be free from the position of a senior pastor in order to conduct mission outreaches into foreign areas and thereby start new branches of the church. I think this type of vision is in all of those who want to work for the Kingdom of God. It is the restless heart of the inner evangelist that wants to get out there and do great things for the Lord. I saw this mentality in many of my colleagues, where they, having done the spadework for a new church and nurtured it into a successful, self-supporting entity, became restless in the need to do more. In biblical terms, this would have been seen as the work of an apostle: to establish a string of churches that serve the needs of the people.

For Pastor Derek and Elaine, the years of diligent work in the establishment of the Eternal Life Church served as their record of commitment to the lord's work . Pastor Derek once mentioned that I would be the perfect person to take over the main operation while he and Elaine went out to raise new fellowships, with the church's support. This type of talk inculcated a dormant ambition in me, and I looked forward to the day when we would both be able to step up to the plate and move into the ministries fore-ordained for us by God.

*

Disillusioned

I followed Pastor Derek into the office, sat down opposite him, and waited while he shuffled a batch of papers into a pile on one side of his desk. Satisfied that the pile looked neat, he leaned back and clasped his hands behind his head. This did not appear to be the same person who left for the States a month ago, and I pondered the cause of the disconnect between my old friend and I. Whatever the problem, I was eager to know the reason for such an obvious cold-shoulder experience. In the back of my mind the strange thoughts, after my conversation with Pastor Derek's mother-in-law on the day after our exceptional Sunday meeting, circled like a hawk in search of its prey.

"I need to share a change in the way we will be handling operations in the future," he said.

The Bigger Picture

I waited with bated breath as Pastor Derek continued: "While Elaine and I were away, many aspects of how we approach the ministry came to light. I have always allowed you, as my assistant pastor, to be my right-hand man on an equal basis of leadership, but the model Elaine and I were exposed to in America showed us that this is not the correct way to run a ministry. Any organization with two heads is a monster; there should be only one person who calls the shots."

I remained quiet in order to absorb Pastor Derek's words.

"We have learned that to be successful in ministry, the senior pastor's wife should become the right-hand person. So I'm elevating Elaine to the position of Pastor. I will make all decisions regarding the future of the ministry with her."

My heart fell and I ventured a question. "But what will I do? Am I not to be a pastor in the work anymore?"

Pastor Derek looked at me with indifference. "I have decided that you should remain as principal of the school, but the pastoral work will be done by Elaine and I."

This was more than I could assimilate. Ever since I came to know the Lord as my Savior, I daily, focused myself on the fulfillment of a pastoral ministry. I believed God called me to be a minister of the gospel, and my entire identity lay wrapped up in this one pursuit.

"But principal of the school is something I took on at your request. I perform the task because I'm a pastor in the church. A pastor is what God called me to be."

Pastor Derek's face appeared as stone. "I'm sorry you feel that way, but things have changed. You need to take a step back and consider what God is saying to you."

I felt numb. "I'll do that and then get back to you," I said.

I will never forget the feeling of helplessness as I left Pastor Derek's office and returned to my own. My whole world seemed to have come crashing down on my head, and everything worked for appeared to have been in vain. Although I enjoyed being principal of the school, I could not imagine it being my full-time vocation. At this time my future path became clearer to me, something never before contemplated: I needed to start a church and build it into a great work. On the way home, Adeline, who taught the grade ones in the school, detected my preoccupation and asked why I looked so down in the mouth. I told her about my conversation with Pastor Derek.

"What will we do?" she asked.

I shared my thoughts about us starting our own ministry, but her silence signaled disagreement.

"I know this comes as a shock, but we need to hear what God has to say about this whole affair. I feel as though the rug has been pulled out from beneath my feet. Perhaps this is the way God will promote us into higher service for the Kingdom," I said.

Adeline countered. "You can't just walk out and start something new! I would have to find a new job, and we don't want to move now. The boys are about to enter their final year of school."

I thought about the implications for a moment, then an idea formed.

"I'll approach Derek and see if he will support me in starting an outreach in a town that's not too far from here. It will take a fair amount of time to grow a new church, and I don't mind traveling back and forth until the fellowship is big enough to support us. I will continue to do architectural drawings for extra income. The boys will have completed their schooling by the time a move to the new town would be required."

With some reluctance Adeline agreed that a move would be better than staying in a situation which fostered bad blood. The other option available, to accept Pastor Derek's proposal and forgo my pastoral ministry did not sit well at all. A third option of a return to secular, full-time work also appeared untenable. The next day, after a sleepless night spent in contemplation of my future prospects, I arrived at the church office with a plan in mind. A young couple, members of our church who relocated to another city, told their parents of the difficulty experienced in finding a place of worship that suited them. The parents of the young couple in question mentioned this to me during a recent pastoral visit made to their home. I decided to test the waters and placed a call to the couple to ask them if they might like to be a part of a new outreach. It would entail the use of their home as an initial venue. Pastor Derek's decision to be out of the office that day suited me and gave time to hear back from the young couple in the neighboring city. The city, situated in the midst of the Eastern Transvaal coal mine community, hosted an innovative process of oil extraction from coal. I posited that many people would be drawn from other parts of the country to look for work in this city and it provided an excellent prospect for the development of a new church.

Late that afternoon I received word from the couple—they would be delighted to be a part of a new work in their new city, and wanted to know when I could start. I told them it depended on Pastor Derek, and that I still had to speak to him about it. That evening I told Adeline of an open door with respect to our intended church plant. I concluded that Pastor Derek would go for it, because it appeared to me I constituted a threat which he wanted to be rid of, despite the offer I stay on as the principal of the school. In the analysis of the vibe I received from my conversation with him, it became apparent he feared that the people in the church might prefer me as the lead pastor—a difficult situation for both him and I, but not of our own making. I ap-

The Bigger Picture

proached him the following day and explained the tough position his changes had placed me in.

I thought he might be empathetic of my position; another mistake on my behalf.

15: Hold Onto That Calling

Pastor Derek leaned forward and narrowed his eyes. "I know you might feel I have placed you in a tough position, but the fact is, things in life change, and we have to be up to the challenge. Don't forget that God charged me with the establishment of this work, and I'm responsible for the direction it takes."

"But you invited me to be a part of the pastoral team, and now you are declining my further involvement in what I believe to be my calling. Are you afraid that I might be more popular with the people?"

A contemptuous smile darkened his features. "This has nothing to do with popularity. I am responding to what I believe to be the correct model for this ministry. I can understand if you don't want to continue with the school; that is your prerogative. However, if you believe your calling is purely pastoral, then I will see what arrangements I can make within the flow of churches we belong to. There may be a church looking for a pastor, or an assistant pastor."

His words brought me to the idea I had in mind. "I spoke to Mike Joubert yesterday, and asked how his son and daughter-in-law were enjoying their new city. He said they had not been able to find a church like ours, so I took the bull by the horns and asked if they would be willing to host a meeting in their home. I told him that if you and the Joubert children were in agreement, I would start a weekly meeting and see where it goes."

Pastor Derek held my eye for a few moments, then slowly nodded. "It may be a solution. I will be prepared to support you for six months, but after that, you will be on your own as far as income is concerned."

I exhaled a sigh of relief. "Then I'll make preparations for an outreach plan after I have talked to Mike and his wife. I would suggest you find a replacement as Principal for the school, as I will need all my time for visitation and travel."

Pastor Derek raised his eyebrows. "I have already thought of that. Peter Van den Berg will be ideal for the position. As you know, he has done an outstanding job in the oversight of our main learning center."

I left his office with hope in my heart, and called Mike Joubert to tell him it would be a go for a meeting in his son's home. Despite my close friendship with Mike Joubert I didn't share the details of what led up to this change. He thought it strange that I would be leaving the school, but I didn't let on as to the true nature of my position. It wouldn't be long, though, before my removal as a pastor in the work caused ripple effects throughout the church. Many thought Pastor Derek to be strong handed when it came to staff, and it didn't take long for many of the people to voice their opinions. They thought it strange that Elaine would become a pastor, by tradition a position only men filled.

The following Sunday, at the morning meeting, Pastor Derek laid down the new law, based on the model he been taught in America.

Many of the church people felt it a wrong move, and I sensed their anger at the loss of my pastoral ministry. I did my best to pour oil on troubled waters in what appeared to be a fire of resentment toward Pastor Derek. In the week that followed several families left the church, the responsibility for which he laid at my door, but I knew in my heart the fault did not lie with me. I told many of the folk who called to ask why I no longer pastored that my decision to step down came as a result of Pastor Derek's new vision for leadership but many of the people read between the lines. They all felt that Pastor Derek suffered a ministerial jealousy and that his "weaker" pastoral ministry would be exposed should I continue to be involved.

The phenomenal growth experienced by Eternal Life Church, from about three hundred and fifty people to over seven hundred members in a little over three years, resulted from the success of our combined ministries. While I gave Pastor Derek full credit for his initial effort he could not have advanced the membership growth all by himself.

In a way, I felt a sense of loss, cheated out of the fruits of my labor; but the move to start a church from grass roots generated a mild, conciliatory excitement. The two months that followed this decision proved difficult in many ways. On Wednesday evenings, I traveled the hundred and ten kilometers (each way) to deliver a Bible study; and on Sundays, I was back to take a Sunday morning meeting in the Joubert junior's home. We attracted several stragglers who didn't feel they could fit into any of the local churches and who showed evidence of divisiveness. Their ambition, it appeared, to cause controversy about doctrines and spiritual practices by asking fringe questions that detracted from the actual lessons being taught.

One of the ladies in regular attendance, whom I shall call Margaret, tried on a continuous basis to attract male attention by dressing provocatively. She made several attempts to flirt with me, often getting too close for my comfort. Adeline wanted me to run her off, but I felt Margaret's behavior stemmed from a difficult upbringing. I heard from one of the other congregants that she grew up in a sexually abusive home circumstance, knowledge which made it difficult for me to ask her to leave because she needed God's love as much as any other person, perhaps even more so.

Several families from the Eternal Life Church, who had bonded with me over my tenure as the assistant pastor, often made the journey with Adeline and I. These families felt an opposition to Pastor Derek's shift in leadership model and wanted to support me in my endeavor to start the new work. The spiritual terrain appeared hard as we persevered with many outreach attempts in the new city, but to little avail. I began to get the distinct feeling that the move might not have been God's perfect plan for us. Our advertising of a home-group meeting brought sparse results, and after six weeks of perseverance, only a few couples attended the meetings. In the meantime, several families back in our hometown who left Eternal Life Church due to my demotion from the pastoral staff called several times to encourage me in the endeavor, but made suggestions that I seek God's face for clarity. They maintained that Pastor Derek's new leadership model would not succeed in the long term. They also made it clear I should reconsider the venture and seek the Lord for a new direction. No one believed I should leave our city where the Lord clearly placed me for a purpose.

At first, I felt limited conviction that their assumptions bore any semblance of reality. My vision, although shaken by the lack of response to our outreach, still lay in the new city. However, another four weeks of labor in this difficult vineyard began to wear my resolve away. Adeline, tired of the travel, made every excuse to stay at home on the set meeting dates, and the few families who accompanied us from the home city could not always make the trip. One night, my car experienced a tire blowout on the way back home, and our journey almost ended in disaster. A couple, I shall call Ray and Janet, accompanied me on this particular evening. I managed to bring the car to a safe stop, but not without several swerves from side to side as I applied the brakes to slow the vehicle down.

Ray and I changed the wheel and continued on with much thanksgiving, but I began to wonder if God wanted to tell me something. Ray and Janet became close friends with Adeline and I. We spent a lot of time together, and Ray made no bones about the fact that he disliked Pastor Derek's new pastoral model, which in his opinion amounted to a reaction caused by my more acceptable pastoral style. He maintained that Pastor Derek suffered a lack of confidence in his own ministry and his power-hungry attitude would lead the Eternal Life Church into eventual decline. I could not fully accept these points of view, however, because I knew Pastor Derek to be a very confident person, in both his ministry and calling.

One night, another member of Eternal Life Church called to invite Adeline and I for dinner. I shall refer to this couple as Don and Elizabeth, another couple whom I helped with counsel after their marriage ran into difficulties. We accepted the invitation and, along with Ray and Janet (also invited), we sat down to the meal.

The conversation centered on Pastor Derek's changes to the general ministry, as I thought it might. "Do you really think you're doing the right thing by trying to open a work in another city?" asked Don.

I raised my eyebrows. "Why do you ask that?"

Ray jumped into the conversation. "I believe God would have you start a new work right here in our city. There's room for another charismatic fellowship and Derek, as much as he thinks God has given him the keys, does not have a monopoly on the work of the Spirit."

Elizabeth, often outspoken in her well-meaning dialogues, took her turn. "There are quite a few families who have left Eternal Life in the hope you might change your mind about leaving our city. Don and I have decided we want to break ties with Pastor Derek and Elaine, and even if you don't decide to return here, we will find a new spiritual home elsewhere."

I countered. "To start a new work under Derek's nose with some of his ex-congregants is perhaps not the best thing to do."

Ray exploded. "I personally don't care what Derek thinks! He believes he owns the spiritual rights to this city, but only God decides who works in the vineyard! We believe in your ministry and over the past three years, we have come to love you and Adeline dearly. We are prepared to support you should you decide to start up here."

The Bigger Picture

I felt that their words made some sense, and the thought of not having to travel that distance three times every week began to take hold. I know that most legalistically-minded Christians would say this is not an honorable thing to do; however, I weighed it against what Pastor Derek had done to me, and found the scales measured on equal terms. In the face of all the adversity experienced, I began to see a light at the end of the tunnel. I am, after all, human.

The decision to close the work in the new city came the following week, when Joubert junior phoned me.

"Pastor Colin, I am sorry to say that my wife and I have decided to return to our hometown as we both hate this city and can't seem to make any friends. If you are going to continue with the outreach you will need to find a new venue."

We, therefore, had no venue to continue the work in. Don and Ray's proposal now made all the sense in the world. I owed it to Pastor Derek to inform him of the status quo, and I knew it would have drastic consequences for the support I received from Eternal Life Church. My financial base would end immediately.

The following morning, I paid Pastor Derek a visit.

16: Categories of Christian Believers

With great respect for religious academia, who might give their own reasons as to why Christians vary in their responses to life in the Spirit, I would like to offer my own opinion on the subject. We serve Christ with a passion that is derived from our character and personality. Average believers seek to serve to a level that will equal their spiritual convictions. In this allusion, the spiritual aspect of life is secondary to life's normal secular pursuits, and church attendance will be based more on convenience than necessity. This does not mean they are weak-minded people who don't care for the deeper aspects of belief but the problem is that they seldom seek deeper to improve their spiritual understanding.

In my experience, the first category of a believer is one who maintains a basic belief only for the benefit of family and friends and doesn't get involved in the church other than through occasional attendance. A second category is an average believer who makes an effort to live a life in accordance with scriptural values. This type of believer will attend regular church meetings, plus find an involvement in the church curriculum. A third category, while in keeping with the second, also places his/her life entirely into God's hands, and spiritual pursuits come before anything else. This third category of believer will have a hard time prioritizing family concerns above church matters because she/he believes God will take care of any objections which may arise out of family circumstances. I believe it is out of this third category that the church derives its full-time ministers.

Another characteristic of this last category is that ministerial service is of a higher intensity than the other two, and will lead to a deeper scrutiny of the belief system. Over long-term service, many of those in this category will question the basis for their belief because they teach others, and it is necessary to believe that one is "rightly dividing the Word of truth." I make these observations because I place myself in this final category of believer.

In my case, all these observations stem from long-term involvement with the ecclesiastic order: almost forty years of church service, of which nineteen years have been spent in a full-time capacity as the shepherd of several flocks. This total experience includes approximately 2,500 sermons preached, inclusive of Bible studies, plus a multitude of weddings and funerals, both which required the relevant officiation, not to mention the hours of spiritual counsel spent with families and individuals on every sort of problem imaginable. I'm not saying I'm an expert, but my observations are all based on long-term and sound experience.

I broach this matter because it's this third category of person who will feel the weight of the many inconsistencies between what is preached, what is practiced and what relates to reality. This is not an indictment against preachers or those who try to adhere to Scriptural principles. I believe it is an indication of the manner in which the individual contemplates change, and how that change will take place within the soul in order to affect a complete and life-lasting transition to righteousness. A scripture literalist is likely to believe that God's presence in the soul of a human being is sufficient to prevent that soul's unrighteous behavior. Real life, however, has shown that even those who have received Christ are still capable of doing bad things, wrong thoughts, and the entertainment of fear.

In my ministerial tenure at Eternal Life Church, I had begun to experience the pain of difficult decision-making. The challenge I faced after Pastor Derek's decision to remove me from the pastoral ministry lay in one of two possible directions; obedience to my senior pastor or obedience to what I believed to be my calling. Obedience to my senior pastor meant an end to my pastoral ministry, while obedience to my calling meant breaking away from the security the church offered me in the form of employment and opportunity. After much serious prayer and consideration, I came to the conclusion my calling as a pastor rated higher than any other.

The Bigger Picture

Pastor Derek must also have faced the same conflict of emotions when he decided to remove me from ministry. From the start, because of our friendship, he allowed the relationship to become a partnership; and for three years, the church thrived and prospered under our leadership. A new scenario confronted him in the form of a different model of leadership, and change became inevitable . This is, as the chief shepherd of a congregation, his prerogative. In hindsight, I believe his approach for a solution lacked consideration of potential consequences; however, this is perhaps something all leaders are guilty of at one time or another, myself included.

Another mitigating factor which I believe bedeviled Pastor Derek's attempts to solve the problem lay in his fear that his position as senior pastor might be usurped by one whom the congregation thought more capable. I am definitely not saying I thought myself to be more capable than he, because I did not know a more capable person for the position. This fear, however, might have played a huge role in his decision to go about it the way he did. It is possible we both suffered from an inability to let go of our fears.

The morning that followed the evening meal with Don and Elizabeth, I reluctantly made my way to the church for a meeting with Pastor Derek. The sudden change in the dynamics of our relationship, that of good friends who enjoyed a fruitful partnership to that of employer and employee, became palpable. But for an occasional request for a report on my progress, our conversations became nonexistent. With two months of my new initiative elapsed, I knew he expected results, but I possessed nothing but apparent failure to report. We sat opposite each other with tangible uneasiness.

"So, how is the outreach coming along?" he asked.

I took a deep breath and thought about my answer. "It has been a bit of a roller coaster. The Jouberts have been very accommodating, but the spiritual ground in the town is very hard, and we have not been that well received by the community."

Pastor Derek leaned back in his chair and observed me through narrowed eyelids. "How many new people have you had contact with?"

I told him about two couples who showed an interest, along with several singles who appeared to be angry with a local pastor. "Both couples seemed to be looking for something specific in worship, and I gathered they're not into the charismatic scene. The few singles, who all knew each other, were angry about the way their ex-pastor had treated them."

"Welcome to church planting, Brother," said Pastor Derek. I steadied my breathing to tell him about my new plan.

"The Jouberts have decided to move back here; he said he resigned, but I think he might have been fired. This means we no longer have a venue."

The Bigger Picture

Pastor Derek frowned. "What do you intend to do?"

"The travel is expensive, and I'm racking up a large mileage on my car. I have been in prayer about a new direction."

He raised his eyebrows and waited for me to elaborate.

"I have decided to start up a new work here in the city," I said.

A dark cloud seemed to fill the room, and I saw the muscles in Pastor Derek's jaw tighten. "You're considering starting a new work on our doorstep? You realize I can't support you if that's what you intend to do?"

I tried to counter. "I don't see why we can't develop a spirit of cooperation. This city is wide open for another charismatic church, and we did so well together until you changed things."

I could feel my ire rising. It became evident to me that Pastor Derek considered the city to be his God-given turf, and did not want to entertain the idea of any competition.

He stood to indicate the end of our meeting. "I'm giving you official notice that your services are terminated, and you will be paid up to today. Any other financial benefits you've been receiving will be terminated forthwith."

"If that is your decision, I understand," I said.

Pastor Derek gave me a dark look. "...and don't think of taking any of Eternal Life's people."

That was the last time I ever spoke to him. At the age of forty-four years I stepped into the realm of the unemployed—the only dismissal from a job in my entire working career.

The trip home seemed to take forever, no doubt due to the contemplation of my precarious future. On my arrival home Adeline, already prepared for this eventuality, accepted the status quo with a nod of her head and we embraced each other for what seemed an interminable period of time. I called Ray and Janet to inform them of my formal dismissal by Pastor Derek and we decided to meet later that evening to plan a new outreach. I possessed little in the way of savings, but did have some income due from the drawing of private house plans. I also contacted Don and Elizabeth to see if their offer of a home for a temporary venue still remained on the table. Word spread like wildfire. Over the next forty-eight hours, I fielded about thirty calls from concerned members of the Eternal Life Church. A few of the callers not only wished me well, but wanted to attend our first meeting when it convened. I told these folk that they had better pray before such a move, as it would cause a lot of trouble with Pastor Derek.

I admit that the whole scenario caused a mental conflict to rise within me. Despite the fact that Pastor Derek chose to distance himself from us, I felt bereaved of a long-standing friendship. Pastor Derek's unsolicited animosity weighed heavily on me, and I made desperate attempts to come to terms with it.

The Bigger Picture

A businessman and good friend of mine called to offer a week of solitude at his vacation cottage, a wonderful gesture of concern for my wellbeing. "It will help you get things sorted out in your mind," he said.

I accepted the gesture, and my friend took a week off while his business partner picked up the slack. His son and one of the twins decided to accompany us so we took off while Adeline held the fort. We spent a wonderful week of peace and quiet at a beautiful area on the South-east Coast; the boys swam in the sea while my friend and I speculated about the future, enjoyed a nightly barbecue, and prayed together. On our return, another businessman, also a member of the Eternal Life Church, called to say he wanted to discuss a possible business venture which would help bring in some finances to supplement my drawing income.

Two months prior, Adeline left her position as a grade one teacher in the school and took up employment with a local veterinary surgeon, also a member of the church, so we had a measure of stability in finances; but more would be needed. This businessman managed a stone quarry on the outskirts of the city, and said his company required someone to clean all their buildings and offices on a regular basis. I set up a small business to employ several ladies to do the cleaning under my supervision. The quarry manager also gave me a contract to draw up plans for all the buildings situated on the quarry grounds, a stipulation by the local municipality for the business to continue under its existing license. These new income arrangements provided additional financial security and allowed me to concentrate on building the new fledgling church.

Things came together for us, but at the same time a war of nasty accusations erupted, and every Christian in the city sensed the bitterness of the breakdown between Pastor Derek and myself. While the excitement of a more viable endeavor lit up my spiritual landscape the dark cloud of the split hung like a pall over all of those involved.

17: The Prosperous Image Perception

Pastor Derek's words came to me via one of the Eternal Life Church members, who approached him with regard to my dismissal: "Colin is going totally against God's will and he will utterly fail."

Not a day went by that I didn't hear some remark about my disobedient spirit, however, I refused to be sucked into the name-calling storm, and did my level best to keep a balanced outlook; but the continuous barrage of remarks hurt. Our new outreach started with about eleven people, and grew quickly as news got around. When folk left Eternal Life Church for whatever reason, they would end up on our doorstep; not a great way to grow the numbers, but one we accepted. I tried not to think about the strong barrage of rhetoric with regard to these defections and the conclusion Pastor Derek drew from them. It appeared he wanted people to see me as a pariah, a devil in Christian clothing, who did everything in his power to draw people away from their home churches.

While movement of members between churches with similar doctrinal pursuits is fairly commonplace, pastors do not try to coerce people away from their home fellowships for good reason. It shows a lack of integrity on the minister's behalf. There is all too often a lack of solid ground as to why members leave their spiritual homes for another. What pastors often don't understand is that there are many different reasons why congregants might seek a change in fellowship. It could be the style of worship they don't like, or overbearing elders. A change in leadership style is another strong advocate for desertion, and I believe that Eternal Life Church manifested this very symptom. Pastors take defections as a personal affront to their ministry, and in this case, I believe I became a scapegoat when several families decided to leave Eternal Life due to the change of leadership model. I heard that some defectors cited the appointment of Elaine as co-pastor to be a conflict of interests that allowed Pastor Derek to push his agendas. They felt there were too few checks and balances, especially in such a large church where a huge amount of money poured in every month.

Another aggravation for the more money-driven members arose due to the fact that Pastor Derek never disclosed a complete breakdown of expenditure. This practice placed the financial expenditure under suspicion, perhaps an unfair sentiment. I never felt that Pastor Derek's motivation lay in the accumulation of personal wealth, or received the impression that anything dubious took place with the church expenditure, however, whenever a family left Eternal Life Church to attend our meetings, I would hear about the "money" story.

The Bigger Picture

Pastor Derek created this impression through the way he kept all the cards close to his chest. Dealing openly with non-profit income and expenditure is a prime characteristic of good stewardship. This principle is something I learned in the aftermath of my dismissal from Eternal Life Church. In our new church I made sure our secretary posted a balance sheet on the local notice board where everyone could see it. No one ever questioned our church expenditures because every month they could view a full report of our fiscal management.

The general charismatic model of church operation is based heavily on the apostolic leadership of one man, who supplies the vision and who will be seen as a sort of supreme leader. He will be expected to initiate all facets of the church's operations and governance through a group of elders, more commonly called assistant pastors in the charismatic model. This is the way Pastor Derek taught me to run a church, and in hindsight I realized that our emulation of some very large charismatic fellowships that boasted memberships in the thousands, became the motivation for us both to believe God approved of this model. We looked up to these ministers, in awe of the way they ran their institutions. In the back of our minds, numbers and finances became the criteria for success. This model originated in the United States around 1965, and swept the world in the latter part of that century. The model differed from that of my previous denominational involvement, where the elders most of whom retained their secular jobs, ran the church. Most of these earlier denominational fellowships never grew beyond fifty people, and the minister, considered as an itinerant preacher who would move on at some future date, provided spiritual guidance, while the elders governed.

Ego plays a large part in the charismatic movement, although for obvious reasons those who are still involved in this type of ministry would never admit to it. Many pastors in our group lacked the charisma and organizational abilities required to facilitate a dynamic growth in their churches and all looked to the large successful works as their example. I remember attending a convention at one of the very large churches in Johannesburg, where a visiting speaker told us first impressions of a pastor went a long way to draw people to a church. He encouraged pastors to live in the best houses, drive expensive cars, and dress like millionaires. The speaker maintained that God's business should always be prosperous in every way possible, and God always provided the best for his children. Anything that displayed less than God's best provided a poor testimony of God's provision. This became known as the "prosperity movement"—the "Name It and Claim It" mentality, where church growth and strong finances solicited the highest priority.

The growth of our fellowship soon presented me with a new need: a bigger venue. We moved the meetings out of Don and Elizabeth's home to a strip mall, where I managed to get a month-to-month deal on office space rental. The second floor offices and assembly space of the largest building in the mall provided an outside entrance of its own and I believed it perfect for our purpose. For the first year, I drew no income from the church, but managed to support our home budget from the proceeds of the cleaning business and the drawing of house plans. The tithes that came into the church coffers through our weekly Sunday morning and evening meetings paid the rent, plus the purchase of chairs, pulpit, tables, and other miscellaneous items used in the ministry.

I soon became very busy and all preparation for the ministry took place in the evenings. My daughter, Alison, taught piano in the year that followed her matriculation and it is ironic that a couple involved with Eternal Life Church offered to pay for her to attend a missionary college in the North-Eastern area of South Africa. I still had many friends in Pastor Derek's church who didn't share his opinion of me but still stayed on board with his ministry. I would sometimes receive anonymous financial gifts in the mail which I assumed came mostly from these families, who despite Pastor Derek's rumble about my spiritual infidelity still wanted to see me succeed.

The twins, Paul and Andrew, while in completion of their final year at the local high school made me proud by taking part-time jobs at a local restaurant where they earned good money from tips, enough to keep themselves in clothes and incidentals.

They understood the problem posed by our limited income and never asked me for money to buy anything they could themselves afford. Alison also showed this type of understanding for our financial plight while she earned money from her music. I owe my three children more than I could ever repay for this type of consideration, and as a father should, I respect and love them to bits. I also know the whole exercise made our family pull together, and my children learned valuable principles which have stood them in good stead to become the fine people they are today.

We soon reached the point where I needed to consider the balance of my time between the growth of the ministry and the provisions of my own income. It became evident to all of us involved that in order for the church to become financially viable, it would require much more input from me. More visitation plus planned outreach endeavors, a Bible study during the week, and a night for prayer were all necessary requirements to facilitate a sustained growth. My closest friend, Ray, became the first appointed elder in the work; and his wife Janet joined me in the cleaning business, thanks to a new contract with a large foreign corporation. I also came up with a brainwave that saved the church a good deal of money on the rent at the strip mall.

An approach to the headmaster of the boy's high school resulted in the use of the school's assembly hall for our Sunday meetings, our financial commitment for this new arrangement a fraction of what the church paid in the mall. In order to facilitate the weekday meetings our bible study and prayer time moved into various homes supplied by members of the congregation. This also, with permission, permitted me to draw some income from the tithes and scale down my architectural drawing practice.

One morning in October 1989 while in preparation of the Sunday sermon, I received a visit from two Christian brothers. I knew the one person well, as he once fellowshipped at Eternal Life Church, but due to a fallout with Pastor Derek, he left about a year prior to my dismissal. I remember this brother's major issue lay in the lack of financial report by the E.L.C's executive, a weak point in Pastor Derek's leadership style. At times when a major project expenditure arose it made its way into a monthly church newsletter but provided limited information. The second person I knew by reputation, as he ran a Christian Video Library from his home. Their church fellowship, the local Pentecostal assembly and longtime feature of the cities religious skyline, served as the original contact group where Pastor Derek rose to some prominence before he fell out with the group's Apostle and left under a cloud to start Eternal Life Church.

I greeted the two gentlemen, surprised that they wanted an audience with me; we moved into the sitting room and after the exchange of a few pleasantries the person whom I knew from the Eternal Life Church addressed me.

"Pastor, Colin, we wanted to run a possible opportunity by you. I know you to be a man of integrity, and to have Pastor Derek malign you in the way he has grieves our hearts, believe me. As you well know, I have been on the receiving end of his wrath, so I can sympathize greatly with you."

I nodded. "I remember the incident and was saddened when you left. What is this opportunity you speak of?"

He leaned forward. "The assembly we attend has run into some difficulties with leadership. As you know, the pastor recently left for another calling, and there has not been anyone suitable with relevant experience of our group. We are an autonomous body under the covering of the Assembly of True Believers, but they have no one to send us at this time. We thought you might be interested in combining your new outreach with our church to provide the leadership."

I was taken aback, and for a moment I didn't know what to say. "What made you think of me?" I asked.

The other brother responded. "Well, Ronnie here says he really enjoyed your ministry when he fellowshipped at E.L.C and you were at one time a part of our group of churches. We see the success you have achieved with your new venture so far, and we feel our church could benefit from your leadership."

I wanted to know more, as the idea intrigued me. "What is your present leadership setup?" I asked.

The Bigger Picture

The other brother continued. "Ronnie and I are the lead elders in the work. We have a retired schoolmaster whom we thought might be able to run the situation, but he feels he is too long in the tooth. I suggested to Ronnie that we approach you."

We spoke for another hour, and they finally stood to leave. "I'll have to put this to my congregation first. I will be in touch," I said.

I phoned Ray at work and shared the opportunity with him. "They have ten acres of ground with a building and about fifty people," I said.

Ray endorsed the potential move with immediate enthusiasm. "It will mean you can become fully supported, and there's a lot we can do with ten acres of ground."

I concurred. "We need to put this to the congregation. If we all agree, then Ronnie will have a meeting with their group's area representative, and it will be put to their congregation. I believe this is God's way of honoring all our hard work."

For me, a new day and a fresh vision were about to unfold, and my most fulfilling time of ministry lay ahead.

18: The Combination of Two Fellowships

After several meetings with the church and the two leading elders, we combined the two congregations, and our first meeting attracted about two hundred people, which included many inquisitive visitors. Ronnie and the other elder gave me carte-blanche, and said they would be willing to step down in favor of new appointments if I so chose. I made the choice to keep them both on as elders and in addition, I appointed another brother from our congregation together with Ray, and convened a meeting to set the parameters for the future. Two different models of leadership and worship style needed to find common ground. The Pentecostal way is somewhat more conservative than the charismatic, but I soon discovered that most of the Assembly people wanted a change. We introduced our music group, plus the clapping of hands to the music, and the most controversial aspect for Pentecostal believers: "dancing in the spirit."

A few disgruntled people, unable to make the transition, left the church, but our unique establishment drew new families, and the church entered a period of growth similar to that during my tenure with Eternal Life Church. Our income sky-rocketed, and I no longer needed to draw on my architectural income, or the proceeds from the cleaning business. I kept the cleaning business going, however, and used its income as a tithe toward the church. Our numbers grew beyond three hundred members, and it did not take me long to get into construction mode. The church building, too small to accommodate the increase in membership, required an extensive expansion program. In keeping with the idea of prosperity, I sold my old Cressida and leased a new BMW 3 series. Pastor Derek's purchase of a late-model Mercedes from one of his congregation members set the tone for the perception of our city's people and although my new car was not as swanky, I felt determined not to be outdone. I think Pastor Derek and I both fell victim to the ploy that success lay in a competition for greater numbers of people and finance—perhaps more me than him.

I look back on those times, all those years ago, and realize what a deep wound my dismissal from E.L.C caused to the city's spiritual community. My defensive strategy, however, lay in the proof of my personal integrity, leadership ability and verbal constraint with regard to Pastor Derek's character. By the testimony of those who left his church to join ours, he did not hold back any punches whenever the opportunity arose in his sermons. While he made no mention of my name, reference would often be made of the "spirit of disobedience that caused the Eternal Life Church a great deal of trouble and threatened to derail his ministry." In retrospect I see the ghost of my father's rejection rear its ugly head yet again in my life, a reminder that no matter what I did it would never go anywhere. I eventually came to terms with the breakup between Pastor Derek and myself, but never fully overcame the trauma of the loss of our friendship. That neither of us could bury the hatchet said much for our lack of maturity in terms of Christian principles . Instead, it became an uneasy stage for finding fault; and as much as we both tried to get on with our respective ministries, the stigma of the split turned both of us into competitors and enemies. The whole debacle made me wonder if we as Christians really experienced a change of nature when we received Jesus as savior, or whether we all just fooled ourselves by means of a strong conviction, a trick of the mind. One can whitewash the leopard, but the spots still remain.

Despite the war that raged between the two of us, the new endeavor with the Assembly brought on a wonderful period of growth and a kaleidoscope of experiences for Adeline and I. The marriage between my daughter, Alison, and my future son-in-law, Mike, took preeminence after my inauguration as pastor of the new church initiative. The couple met at the Africa School of Missions and fell in love. Mike, a native of Texas, USA, and the product of a Christian school, sought to learn about, and be involved in missions, by coming to South Africa. When their two-year missionary course ended at the end of 1989, Alison returned home to us with Mike in tow. Meanwhile the twins, after completion of their final year at school, engaged in college level studies, neither yet certain of a career direction. The church, which we renamed New Beginnings Christian Fellowship, continued to grow in membership, and we established four strong home groups that convened every Wednesday night. I appointed Ray to oversee the music group, and we purchased the latest music equipment for their use.

One of the ladies in our church, a school teacher whom I shall call Mary-Anne, approached me one day with an idea. "We should start a school to help the indigenous people with their education. I have been approached by some families to see how you would feel about it."

I knew the answer to the question without even giving it a thought. "I think it's an excellent idea. However, it will take a huge amount of finance to put up the buildings. We have all the ground we need for a fair-sized school."

Mary-Anne's eyes lit up. "I think you're the ideal person to head up such a project! The two families who approached me have their children in attendance at the Catholic school, but the intake of children is very limited. They have tried to get their kids into Pastor Derek's school, but it's full. Both fathers of the children work at a local factory owned by a large American consortium, and believe that if they approach their superiors, finances could be made available to help establish a school."

The factory of which she spoke happened to be the same institution where I held a cleaning contract. "Let them know I'm interested," I said. "If enough money is made available, I'll be able to save costs by running the entire building project myself."

In addition, Mary-Anne provided more news: "I know of four other teachers who will definitely leave the National Department of Education for the opportunity to work for a private concern."

The idea generated a great amount of enthusiasm amongst the elders and the congregation, so we set up a separate fund to save money for the project. I met with Mary-Anne to discuss the curriculum and we decided not to use the Accelerated Christian Education system, but provide a normal government-approved curriculum to be delivered in a Christian environment. I felt confident we were able to finance the initial building construction of the washrooms and at least two classrooms to begin with. Mary-Anne would be appointed as the school's first principal while I took on the role as administrator. She became responsible for the teaching staff, relevant salary structure and decisions on the purchase of school equipment, while I worked on the cost of the building project and the legalities of registration as an educational institute.

A few days later, someone knocked on my office door, a man, dressed in a suit. "Pastor Setterfield? My name is Isaac Khumalo, and I work for Cyanamid Incorporated. Some of our workers have been talking in glowing terms about your church and what you want to do for black education."

We shook hands and he sat down opposite me. I asked the office secretary to make us each a cup of coffee, and exchanged a few pleasantries with Mr. Khumalo.

"The project is already underway," I said. "It's not my first time of involvement with building a school, but it will take a fair amount of time to accomplish. I have limited finances I can put forward to get it going."

Mr. Khumalo smiled. "I had a long talk with Mary-Anne, whom I know because she teaches at the Catholic school, and I think you will be interested to see what is in this envelope."

He pulled a white envelope from his jacket pocket and placed it on the desktop. "Please feel free to open it and have a look. I'm sure you will be pleasantly surprised."

Intrigued, I opened the envelope and found a cheque inside. The amount of the donation nearly blew my mind. Words stuck in my throat, and I looked at Mr. Khumalo's smiling face. "You have got to be kidding me! This is a huge amount of money," I said.

"It is no joke, Pastor. I have spoken to the directors of our company, and as you know, it is an American consortium with factories all over the world. They are also aware of the government regime's insipid policy toward the education of our people, and are prepared to donate another amount in six months' time."

I felt giddy with excitement. "I can build the entire school for that amount!" I said.

"Perhaps you will be able to increase the size of your school, Pastor. Our entire local workforce is prepared to support it—that will mean over two hundred children."

I stared at him in disbelief. "I will upgrade our planning immediately. What are your requirements for us to access this money?"

"I am not laying down any requirements. By reputation, I know you are a man of your word; and if you say this school will be built, that is good enough for me. My superiors will ask for updates from time to time."

He left me in a state of high jubilation. I called Mary-Anne and then Ray to let them know about the miracle. I speculated that the entire school would be ready to receive students within six months. The washrooms would be built first, and with the completion of each classroom, we could take in children to fill them. That way, the school could get going as soon as the local and educational authorities gave their approval. The news traveled quickly, and by the next day, the entire congregation knew about the donation. We took it as a sign of God's approval, and a short while later, I drew up all the plans for the local authority to consider.

Mary-Anne drew up the school's documents of registration, and two other teachers, members of our congregation, helped her set up the curriculum. We decided that the school should cater from grade one to standard six (grade eight) levels to begin with. Six months prior to this event, we built a creche for children between the ages of three years and five years, and it ran at full capacity under the auspice of a qualified congregation member. I struggled to believe the speed with which things came together.

One month later, we received a visit from an officer of the Department of Education, who spent a day going through all the details with regard to the curriculum. I showed her the building plans, already passed by the local municipal authority, and she voiced her satisfaction with the entire project. Our country's racially charged system appeared to be crumbling away as church schools took on the business of education. No one asked me about the race, color or creed of our patrons whereas a few years before, when I did all the applications for Pastor Derek and the E.L.C school, the head of the Education Department grilled me for an hour. His question at the time, and I quote: "What the hell do you think you are doing? school education should be the government's official business, not the church's.

You should not be offering this level of education to the black population."

Pastor Derek's school took in students of all races and this, I believe, with Nelson Mandela's imminent release from prison, went a long way toward the sudden change of attitude by the apartheid authorities. I believe they saw the writing on the wall for official segregation.

Mary-Anne arrived at my office one afternoon with five other ladies in tow. "These ladies are all Christians, and would love to have an opportunity to teach at the school," she said.

"I'll leave all the staff requirements up to you," I responded. "I have enough on my plate right now, what with all this building work coming up, and I still have to run the church on top of it all."

A week later, the project entered full building mode. I hired a competent contractor to start the foundations and ordered all the required building materials. Every Sunday morning, before and after the service, the congregation monitored the construction's progress, happy to be a part of a venture that normalized education for our indigenous peoples. Shortly after that, several families, all from the Cyanamid factory, paid our fellowship a visit, and the church's membership increased by at least another twenty people.

The Bigger Picture

Church meetings and life continued on, but not without some problems on the building site and from some members of the congregation. One Monday morning on my arrival at the office I received some unpleasant news from our contractor.

Colin Setterfield

19: The Ups and the Downs

Our building contractor, Skankwan (which in the vernacular means a wooden peg), approached me with a downcast look in his eyes. "Pastor, Colin, the skebengas (thieves) have stolen all our steel window frames."

The bad news came on the heels of two wonderful Sunday meetings with record attendances and meaningful worship. The building project attracted a lot of interest from members of the community, many of whom paid a visit to view our progress. The steel window frames, purchased on the Friday and stored in our materials shed, awaited installation that Monday morning and we could not be sure if the theft took place on the Saturday night or Sunday after the evening meeting. "How many frames were taken?" I asked.

"All of them, Pastor. They were chained together and padlocked to make it difficult to steal, but it looks as though they carried the whole bundle out."

The Bigger Picture

"Have you looked to see if they aren't on the property somewhere? With the gates locked, it wouldn't have been possible for them to bring a truck in to transport the frames."

"I will send two of my guys to search the rest of the property," said Skankwan.

The church building with flower gardens, car park, and driveway took up one-fifth of the ten acres; the rest of the property lay covered with knee-high grass. Ten minutes later, Skankwan came back with a jubilant look on his face. "We have found the frames, Pastor! The skebengas probably did not have a truck, and found the whole bundle too heavy to carry, so they dumped it near the fence, by the road! They may intend to return for it tonight."

I thanked God for His apparent intervention, and we made plans to fortify the shed's door lock; but the next Sunday when the deacon in charge opened the church to set things up for the meeting, he discovered a nasty surprise. A compromised sliding door on one side of the main hall told its own story; the return of the thieves. The audio mixer, microphones, speakers, and drum set could not be found anywhere on the property. For some unknown reason, they did not take the electric piano. I felt violated.

I immediately called a steel fabrication company to instal security gates on all our doors and windows. The local alarm company arrived the next morning and installed a monitored alarm system. Our insurance partially covered the loss, so we dug into our savings and investment money for the purchase of new music equipment. The escalation of crime in the country reached an all-time high after Nelson Mandela's release from prison. This may have been due to the expectancy that the apartheid regime teetered on the verge of collapse and might soften their approach to racial profiling in order to introduce a preamble to change of government. The good people rejoiced, while the bad took it as an opportunity to steal as much as they could.

I turned one of the old office rooms into a baby's cry room with a special one-way window that allowed mothers to look after their babies in a separate area but still maintain a good view of the pulpit, plus hear the sermon. We rigged a special lock for the cry room door and moved all the equipment off the stage for safekeeping after every Sunday night meeting. Another security measure provided two separate rooms, close to the new school construction, which I offered as a free accommodation to the two groundsmen in the church's employ. The two men jumped at the opportunity to have accommodation on-site, which meant they did not have to make the journey each day from the local township on the outskirts of our city. One of the men, Ben, in his fifties, lived in the township with his young family; the other, a twenty-one-year-old from the Transkei, lived on his own in one of the township's notorious hostels. I expected this move would also resolve the theft problem, which it did.

One Sunday evening during our worship time, Ray touched my shoulder and beckoned me to follow him toward the back of the hall. We passed through into the church's foyer where a man I knew well, Mary Anne's brother-in-law, Fred Harms, waited for me. Fred suffered alcoholism as did his brother, Mary-Anne's husband, Aiden. Aiden, an electrical contractor, spent much of his profits on drink. His brother, Fred, worked as an artisan in the business when sober.

By his unsteady motion Fred's inebriation became apparent, and I wondered why he required an audience at that specific moment. We entered my office and I motioned him to sit in the seat opposite so that the desk would be between us. In an effort to discern his intentions, I took my seat, in expectation he would do the same, but he remained standing. I leaned back in my chair, and waited for him to elaborate. With a sudden lurch forward, he placed his hands on the desk and stuck his chin out at me. I discerned by the unsteadiness and slur in his voice that our conversation might become interesting. Ray hesitated to leave us alone but someone needed to make sure the church worship continued a little longer while I dealt with this problem. Ray nodded at me and closed the door on his departure.

Fred's eyes flamed blood-red and his demeanor became hostile as he thumped the desk with his one fist. "You're a f..... coward, not a f.... pastor!" he shouted.

I was taken aback. "Why do you say that?"

"You told Merle to have nothing to do with me! What right have you got to interfere in my relationships?"

I realized the cause of his angst. Merle, a divorced lady in our church, approached me for advice a few days prior to the service. She complained that Fred's numerous attempts to get her into bed made her feel uneasy about his intentions. My advice, based on prior knowledge of Fred's lifestyle, resulted in Merle's withdrawal from the relationship.

I made my position clear. "Fred, you are bothering a lady who doesn't want anything to do with you. I told her that if you didn't leave her alone she should get a restraining order."

Fred's facial features hardened. "You have no right to f..... interfere. I'm going to show you what happens when you cross Freddy Harms."

I detected an imminent escalation of Fred's hostility toward me. He lunged across the desktop, but anticipation saved me from the punch which would have landed in my face. In one quick movement I pushed my chair back, away from the desk and jumped onto my feet. At the same time, I shouted at him. "I rebuke you in the name of Jesus Christ! If you continue on this path, God will deal with you!" I pointed my finger at him and prepared to keep the desk between us should he come after me.

My words impacted Fred with dramatic effect. I knew he and his brother, Aiden, brought up in a Christian home, understood the principles of good conduct taught by the church and both possessed a good knowledge of the Bible. For someone to accuse them of being anti-Christ would register high on the guilt scale.

Fred stopped in his tracks and swayed back and forth with a mortified look on his face, as a sudden realization of the ramifications struck home. I could still hear the sound of worship coming from the hall. The thought crossed my mind that he might try to keep me in the office, and I prayed for Ray to return and check on my safety. Fred swayed and fell over sideways into the chair which he previously shunned. He placed his hands over his face and began to moan. Tears breached his fingers as he broke out into sobs of frustration.

In a meek voice, he spoke. "I'm so sorry, Pastor. I didn't mean to come here and act like this. I've been drinking too much lately."

In relief, I sat down again. "I'm not your enemy, Fred, but drink will definitely lead you down the path to hell. You know that. You're better than this."

Fred nodded in agreement. "I should go home and let you get on with the meeting," he said. With all the rage dissipated Fred stood slowly to his feet and hung his head in shame. "I'm so sorry I shouted at you," he said. "I'm not a bad person."

I came around the desk and embraced him. "I know you're not a bad person, Fred. You must, however, get your act together, or things will only get worse."

"Can I come and see you tomorrow?" he asked.

"I will expect you at 9:30 am. You really need to come back to church and start serving the Lord again," I answered.

At that moment, Ray opened the office door and peered into the room. "Everything okay?"

"Everything is just fine. Fred is leaving for home to sober up," I said. "He will come back and see me for counsel tomorrow morning."

Fred lived in a rented house directly across the road from the church premises, so he didn't have far to go. At the main entrance doors, he turned and placed his hands on my shoulders. The smell of liquor on his breath almost overwhelmed me. He then staggered down the steps and weaved his way along the driveway to the road.

The worship period ended as I walked back into the hall and stepped up to the pulpit. My knees still felt a bit shaky, but the adrenalin surged as I opened the Bible and announced the verse of scripture to support my sermon.

The Bigger Picture

Fred never did come back the next day. I think the shame of his actions, once soberness set in, became too much for him to bear. I dropped in at his house later in the afternoon, but he would not come out to talk, so I left it at that. The next Sunday, when we started the morning service, Fred opened the doors and windows of his home and set his stereo on full blast for the whole neighborhood to hear. I think his actions stemmed from another bout of drinking. I saw a police van parked in his driveway after the conclusion of our church meeting, and guessed that a report from one of the neighbors resulted in their presence. Fred's attempt to disturb our meeting ended in failure.

I turned to Ray and said, "There's never a dull moment in the ministry is there?"

20: Mrs. Promiscuous

For the next two years, the church grew steadily to over three hundred members. Due to my heavy workload with the building project and school administration the elders helped out whenever I needed a short break from preaching. Mary-Anne proved to be a competent school principal, and with more than two hundred children, she had her hands full in supervising the day-to-day activities. New Beginnings Church became the hope for the city's many indigenous folk who could afford the school fees and wanted a good education for their children. According to a family that initially visited Eternal Life Church as a prospective spiritual home, Pastor Derek showed little appreciation for our newfound fame. His reference to New Beginnings Church as an illegitimate baby drove this family to visit us and discover the truth for themselves. They did not return to Eternal Life Church.

Another area of growth happened amongst the ladies of the fellowship. Adeline chose not to be involved in any form of leadership, so I asked the wife of one of the deacons to convene a weekly prayer time for the stay-at-home wives and moms in the church. The deacon's wife did a wonderful job amongst the ladies, all who began to pray and be involved in outreaches to the community. They met every Wednesday in the church hall after the completion of the school's morning gathering. Over the time I built a new office for myself at the back of the church building, where I spent my mornings. When the school day finished at 1:30 pm, I drove home for lunch, then return at 3:00 pm to be available for the counsel of church members.

A new couple whom I shall call Mervin and Sophie visited the Sunday morning meeting and fell in love with the fellowship. Mervin, a mechanic by trade, told us that he and Sophie believed in God's call to help churches with children's ministry, however, the constant pressure of travel, suitable accommodation and lack of finances did little for their health and they wanted to settle down in a permanent spiritual home. Mervin informed me he intended to find a job in our city, and if permitted, he and Sophie could take over our children's Sunday school. I felt a twinge of uneasiness about this couple, as they both came across as "super-spiritual" in their talk, but did not appear to be well grounded in the scriptures. After due consideration I offered a limited involvement with our children's ministry, but under the auspices of the appointed overseers.

Happy with my directive Mervin and Sophie researched homes for rent and started a job search for support of their livelihood. Sophie made good friends with one of the stay-at-home wives in the fellowship, and I understood that an offer of temporary accommodation came from this person until Mervin and Sophie found a home they could afford. The two couples appeared to get on well together, and for the next month, all seemed to be in order while Mervin and Sophie looked for jobs in the city. I noticed that Mervin did not attend the church on a regular basis, but Sophie came for every meeting and soon became a hit with the ladies, who all thought her to be a very spiritual soul. I, on the other hand detected an agenda with Sophie, who appeared to advocate a weird belief with regard to physical and spiritual healing. When in prayer with the ladies she would rub everyone's hands with a hand cream, a symbolic demonstration of the medicinal anointing with oil for healing, an Old Testament practice.

One particular Wednesday when the ladies all filed into the main hall for their meeting, I requested they gather outside on the lawn while I changed a light fitting in the hall's ceiling. The vaulted roof, close to twenty feet off the ground, required a scaffold which I erected beneath the broken light. While busy on the scaffold and about to remove the old fitting, I heard the ladies troop back into the hall and stand in a circle around the base of the scaffold. The prayer group leader called to me. "Please come down, Pastor. We want to pray for you."

I thought it an inconvenient time to make such a request, but didn't want to discourage them. If they felt God wanted me to be prayed over, why should I object? I climbed down and stood next to the scaffold as the ladies approached to lay hands on me.

The Bigger Picture

Sophie stepped forward with her vial of cream and began to apply it to both my hands. They all took turns to pray about each aspect of my leadership, and for protection of my ministry and my family. When Sophie touched my hands to rub on the cream, she lingered; and then squeezed my fingers from time to time while she searched her mind for extra things to pray about. This made me feel uncomfortable; her touch seemed more sensual than spiritual, but I let it go due to the presence of the other ladies. I didn't want to discourage them from doing good deeds.

They completed their mission, thanked me, and returned to the lawn outside, while I concluded the change-over of light fittings. I felt uneasy about Mervin and Sophie, and wondered about their real agenda. Later, I asked their host about his impressions, of the new couple. The husband assured all to be well; that both Mervin and Sophie busied themselves everyday in a search for jobs but could not provide me with any details as to what else the couple did. The host's wife testified to the fact that Mervin and Sophie, indeed went out everyday to look for a home to rent and search for work but I found out later that the she did not tell the whole truth.

About a week later, on a Monday morning, the host paid me a visit, and I detected a deep sadness in his voice. With tears in his eyes he related the sad story to me. It appeared that his wife and Mervin became attracted to one another and that the affair blossomed into a sexual relationship. Whenever Sophie went off to look for work Mervin would return to the home and spend the morning in bed with the host's wife. Suspicious of his wife's sudden coldness toward him, the host returned one morning to discover the awful truth. The host's wife and Mervin disappeared soon after.

I spent many hours in counsel with the host, but his disillusionment drove him to the point of utter despair. After several weeks he resigned his job, sold his home, and left for another city. I blamed myself for the incident because, in the beginning, my gut told me something wasn't right. The fellowship soon picked up on the gist of the infidelity and tongues started to wag at a furious rate. After a discussion with Ray and the other leaders, I decided to make an official statement to the congregation with regard to the unfortunate event and it took several weeks for things to return to normal. We never saw Mervin, Sophie, or the host couple again.

On another Wednesday afternoon, at the end of the school day, the younger of the two groundsmen knocked on the door of my office.

"Pastor, I went into Ben's room to see why he never came back to work in the garden after his lunch. I cannot wake him up. Something is wrong."

Ben, the older of the two, enjoyed an impeccable attendance record since the day of his employment. I knew by the red color of his eye sclera that he abused marijuana from time to time but the occasional use of the weed never detracted from his ability to do his job, so I overlooked this small infringement. I walked across to the groundsmen's facilities and knocked on Ben's door. He did not respond, so I opened the door and peeked inside. Ben, who appeared to be asleep, lay on the bed with his face to the wall. I called to him, but received no response. The younger groundsman entered and said, "I shook him by the shoulder, Pastor, but he wouldn't wake up."

I put my finger to Ben's jugular, but could not feel any form of a pulse, so I tried his wrist. Nothing. I turned to the younger man. "I'm afraid Ben is dead."

The groundsman sucked in a breath and then uttered a grunt of alarm. "He seemed fine this morning."

I raised my eyebrows. "That may well be, but there is no pulse, and his flesh is quite cold to the touch."

"What will we do?" he asked.

"I will have to call the police. They must make sure there has been no foul play. Did you see anyone else go into his room?"

"No one has been in his room, Pastor. I ate my lunch outside on the bench next to the playing field and I never saw anyone. After the schoolchildren all left the premises, I was digging in the garden for two hours when I suddenly realized I had not seen Ben. That's when I knocked on his door. I promise I never touched him, other than a shake on the shoulder to try and wake him up."

The police arrived half an hour later and confirmed Ben's demise. They checked for foul play, but found nothing out of the ordinary. A mortuary van arrived soon after, and carted poor old Ben's body away. I realized I knew nothing about his family. In accordance with apartheid law, the inigenous people could not own property within the city limits, and this meant they had to travel from the townships to their jobs in the city. I always felt this to be a harsh sentence for them, as they needed to rise very early in the morning, catch various buses, and arrived home late in the evenings.

I discovered that Ben's wife and two young children, depended on him for their livelihood. We informed the family of the death, and because she possessed no money for a funeral, I decided to give her a donation from the church coffers. I asked that she come in with the children to see me the next day. The following morning, the entire family trooped into my office, and Ben's father demanded that the money be given to him. I did not trust him. Ben lived in a separate facility with his wife and children, and I could see that if I gave the money to the father he would use it for himself and Ben's wife would not see a cent of it.

I refused to give him the money and the old man wailed about their culture being violated. He said that the head of the family made all the arrangements for these events, and that the young wife would not know what to do. I could see a disconnect between him and the young woman. She appeared to be afraid of the old man, so I told her to wait around while I sent all the other family members away. After the departure of the others I confirmed my suspicions of ben's father; that the old man would have taken all the money for himself. We attended the funeral in the township a week later, which brought the saga to an end.

21: Moving On

As the country approached the advent of Nelson Mandela's release from prison, the mood of the people began to change. The government made all sorts of conciliatory overtures to the indigenous people of the country; too little, too late was the comment from the liberal voices who advocated change for many years. The South African government regime withdrew more and more into its shell, and the hardliners became more vocal. Our school drew some nasty criticisms from the extreme right-wing, who still felt they might be able to control the country's future. The ultra-right group threatened civil war. A few attempts to make political statements against the change brought swift retaliation from the government and most of the people in, and outside, the country condemned the perpetrators with much vigor. I received threats against our church, which we took very seriously. I know that Pastor Derek and Eternal Life Church also received similar threats because of their school; in fact, over the time of my principalship there I received a letter from a group of activists who warned us to discontinue our education project or they would target us.

After Mandela's release in 1990, the right-wing became even more vocal, and I decided to take precautions against the possibility of an attack on our congregation. An organization called the Azanian People's Liberation Army, in opposition to the African National Congress and the Nationalist government, upped the ante with attacks on farmers and threats against any institutions that assisted the political ambitions of other races. In July 1993, a group of four insurgents from APLA attacked the St. James church in Cape Town. They killed eleven worshippers and wounded fifty-eight.

Some months prior, before the theft of the window frames, I installed a six-foot diamond-mesh fence around the perimeter, with a steel entrance gate. On Sundays, a deacon locked the main gates to the grounds after the arrival of all the congregants, and that's how we continued to worship until after the changeover of power to the new ANC government in April 1994. Despite the sentiment that a bloodbath would take place after the elections, and all people of european descent would be massacred, a peace and calm reigned over the country. Many remained optimistic, and some even stated that the new era would bring reconciliation and great prosperity.

About eighteen months prior to the elections in April 1994, I began to have strange emotions with regard to the ministry and my life as a pastor. A plateau in church growth, accompanied by looming changes to the country's political ambiance, caused many businesses to cut back on their staff. Some of our strongest tithers lost their jobs during this period and needed to relocate to other cities for work. The school, on the other hand, reached capacity, and I prepared a further expansion; however, the entire economic state in the country appeared to be in flux. I remember periods of mental conflict about my future, and felt it may be better for me to resign and hand off to someone younger who might have a fresh vision.

One Sunday morning while we were in worship, I looked across the congregation, with their eyes closed and hands raised in the air, and wondered if this represented all the Christian life embraced. There seemed to be something plastic about the regular tone of our worship, the same people coming forward for prayer, the same songs sung at every meeting, and the predictable response to the sermon.

I thought back over the period of my stay in the city, with its constant demand on the lives of everyday people, circumstances that drove good people like the host couple to divorce and people like Fred to alcohol because of some negative event in their lives. My entire learning experience of spiritual matters, from the day I first set foot into the Word of God Church many years earlier, had been guided by the strong hand of religious fundamentalism. A feeling of suffocation gripped my soul. My life appeared to be crammed into a religious box governed by many man-made rules and regulations. Despite the regular affirmation through scripture of the love of God, we all still dealt with the darker side of life. People still committed crimes, they still murdered each other, they still died. The whole cycle of life and death seemed so unfair and absurd to me.

Although I understood God's divine plan of salvation as taught in scripture, there appeared to be several cracks in the apparent wall of fundamentalist interpretation. In hindsight, this negative thought process might have been the precursor of the eventual shift in my belief system. My questions on the matter of scripture begged a greater personal in-depth scrutiny, and I gained an impression that there might be a much bigger picture beneath all the metaphoric jargon—a greater reality, hidden in plain sight, so to speak. I continued to call on God for guidance.

One morning, alone in the church hall while deep in prayer, I believed the Lord asked me a pertinent question: "Can you walk away from all this that you have placed your hand to?" The question shocked me to the core. I was not sure I knew the answer, but I began to get the distinct feeling that it might be time for me to throw myself on God's grace, resign my position as senior pastor, and move on to new pastures.

The jaded view of my calling may have been the result of all the changes in the country, compounded by my father's death in July 1993. My relationship with my Dad had taken a turn two years earlier, when he started to suffer from angina and we suspected a deterioration in his heart condition. Robert and I moved Dad and Doreen out of their Durban Flat (due to high costs of living) in January 1991. We decided it would be better for them to be closer to Robert and I. Vanderbijlpark was about ninety minutes' drive from where I lived, and Dad made the choice to move to Robert's home city. Three months after the move, Doreen passed away and Dad moved into a smaller flat, but he became very depressed, and we feared he might suffer a heart attack while on his own.

I asked Robert if Dad could move in with him, but he declined, so Adeline and I decided it would be our Christian duty to take my father in. It was ironic that the son my Dad thought to be "rubbish," one who would never achieve anything, became the one to step in and provide the old man's security for the final years of his life. Bittersweet. Despite the early times of being treated as a reject, my relationship with my father had improved over the years, and I believe he came to regret his initial opinion of me. I knew that in the end, to complete the family cycle of care for those first charged with the responsibility for your welfare as a child, it would be my role to provide that security for him in his old age.

I took my Dad's funeral service at our church. He faithfully attended every Sunday morning service but would fall asleep shortly after the worship and with his head tilted back, mouth wide open and eyes closed, this became a familiar sight for me as I conducted the service from the pulpit. Too proud to wear hearing aids, and eighty-five years of age, aspects of a senior's life from which we would all suffer, it became incumbent on us to forgive him this small impropriety. Throughout his life I believed him to have been a very good man, blessed with a clever, mathematical mind, and with no propensity toward religion he answered his own life questions from a scientific base.

While happy to fulfill my Christian and family role in the provision of a home for him, it never occurred that the move would pose any difficulties. Dad commandeered the TV remote at every opportunity and no one, other than myself, could take it from him. Eventually to solve the problem I put a second TV in his bedroom. Adeline always felt that he looked down on women, and although he respected her position in the home, he considered himself to be second to me in the hierarchy of family authority. I loved him, but I also felt a measure of anger due to his misogynistic ways and his treatment of Adeline. I understood why my brother and sister-in-law did not want him in their home.

After Dad's death, I went to the funeral home to collect his ashes; and for some reason, still not quite understood by myself, was reticent to bring the urn into our home for storage, but left it in the trunk of the car, where it remained until the interment. The ceremony took place in the garden of remembrance at Robert's place of worship, the Anglican church in Vanderbijlpark. Dad's wishes, that his ashes together with the remainder of my late mother's ashes (purposely left for the occasion after

Dad, Robert and I, in a small, family ceremony, spread a half-vial over a rose garden in Durban) were to be interred there. The ashes of Dad's second wife, Doreen, already interred at the Vanderbijlpark church shared a spot with my mother's. Dad's directions to Robert provided for the three plaques to be set in the garden wall, with his above those of my mother and Doreen. His viewpoint on women remained steadfast to the end.

I believe my anger toward my dad stemmed from his dismissal of Christianity and his dislike for people of color. This, however, did not distract from the duty I felt toward his welfare or my love for him as a parent. I had, however, never once heard him say, at any time, that he loved me; but I think deep down in his heart he came to respect my rise from a "rubbish" to one appointed to a position of responsibility as an engineer in a large corporate industrial company, and then who aspired to become a respected man of God in charge of a viable ministry in the city. It's not that I think I personally achieved anything spectacular, but I certainly did not fulfill his prophecy of doom for my future. While I have certain regrets about some bad decisions made, I feel confident that my life's story leans more toward success than failure.

In August of 1993, Adeline received a call from a couple, good friends from our days in the Assembly of True Believers church, that they might emigrate. At the time thousands of white South Africans felt conflicted about the country's future;

and many began to leave for what they considered to be greener pastures. The first reason focused on the fear of a bloodbath after election day; and the second, that the ANC would not be able to run the country competently, and everyone would face a downturn in the economy with corruption on a basis not previously realized in modern government. This second reason became the foundation for my own decision to consider emigration. With my father gone, I had no obligation to stay if an opportunity arose to seek a new future.

Our friends shared news of a seminar they intended to attend, which catered to those interested in immigration to Canada and they wanted to know if we might be interested. In the conversation that followed Adeline voiced her own fears about South Africa's apparent path of destruction, and the bleak future our two boys faced if we remained in the country. She shared the details of our friend's plans and suggested we join them at the seminar. Despite my prior thoughts about the possibility of emigration I felt conflicted but took the liberty to book our seats at the upcoming seminar.

I knew that, as our closest friends and supporters of the ministry, Ray and Janet would have to be told. Ray and I spoke often about the changing terrain in the country, and he nurtured the idea that he and Janet might one day leave. The next day, I called Ray and told him about our potential plans.

He laughed. "Janet and I have been thinking exactly the same thing. It must be of God. We want to come to the seminar with you."

22: Immigration

Ray and I decided not to let anybody in the church know about the immigration seminar. This evoked a conflict of emotions for Adeline and I, as we never kept anything about our lives secret, but when a sin of omission is committed the reason for information withheld is obvious. The truth will come out in the end and omission is a delaying tactic that tends to limit the effect of the fallout. If the truth of our decision to leave became known, it would devastate many members of the congregation to learn that their pastor planned such a move. It is tantamount to a father who walks out on his children... and this is how some people may have seen it at the time. Our potential emigration if made known, in my mind, placed the church's long-term survival in jeopardy, and I feared some might jump ship in the absence of a plan for my replacement.

Pastor Derek, I'm sure, enjoyed a field day when the news eventually broke. It is difficult to explain the reason for such an action against an entity (the church) you have helped bring into being. The hard facts of the times, however, spoke for themselves. I believed God would take care of any situation that might harm the church, or my reputation.

Another factor pertinent to our decision to leave lay in the notion that my ministry appeared to have plateaued; a change in leadership would rectify the situation and prevent a decline. The continuous verbal warfare waged by Pastor Derek and those close to him also demanded a solution. The problem would be resolved if one of us left the area; plus a fresh vision for our church would find traction under a pastor not embroiled in the past spiritual history of the two churches. It is outrageous that two adults, both strong in the Christian faith, never found a way to bury their differences but I think the terrain of brotherly love between us, once so strong and resolute, became fouled by pride and feelings of betrayal. I had loved and respected Pastor Derek during those first years of our combined ministerial tenure and considered him my closest friend at the time. In his eyes, what he believed needed to be done to rectify the leadership model may have appeared the correct action for the furtherance of the ministry to which he felt a fatherly attachment. The rough-shod way he went about it, however, with little consideration for the real outcome, revealed Pastor Derek's inability to find a more equitable solution. It could have been so different. The only reason I can put forward is his being seriously threatened by the possibility of my ministry eclipsing his. I, in turn, became threatened by his sudden rejection of my ministry.

All these issues, the unprecedented changes in the country, the shaky economics due to the times, the fear of the future, the concern for our children, the plateau in ministry, and the bad blood between Eternal Life Church and us played a huge role in my decision to move on. With our strong and dedicated group of people I did not fear for the survival of the New Beginnings Fellowship in the wake of my departure, and it remained for me to find an appropriate substitute with a fresh vision to take my place.

When our plans to move on became known, the mood in the church changed to a somber outlook of pessimism with regard to our decision; but the congregation's respect and support for us did not waiver. The original Assembly lead elder, Ronnie, who championed my call to the new church, remained supportive to the end and to my knowledge, no members left the church due to our decision to move on. I found a good substitute for my position, the young pastor who some twenty years prior, joined the Word of God Church through the electoral college, our first place of fellowship. His achievement of a Ph.D. in Theology elevated him to the rectorship of the College where I began my own personal studies for the ministry. The greatest benefit to him lay in the fact that he desired a new opportunity to be back in church ministry again, and New Beginnings posed a great potential for future growth under a fresh vision.

I invited the prospective pastor to preach one Sunday morning to gauge the reaction of the congregation toward his leadership. It appeared that most of the congregation liked him; however, the three remaining elders did not. They felt it would be better to give my young assistant pastor the pulpit and let him run things. Young Martin, although a good man with a degree in divinity, possessed little in the way of real leadership ability, and I voiced my opinion with regard to his youth and lack of experience. The remaining elders did not agree and felt they should be the ones to decide who would take over in my place. I conceded to this request. Another change came from Mary-Anne and the school's teachers. They proposed that the school be separated from the church and become financially independent from the New Beginnings ministry. The elders thought this a good idea, so I made arrangements for this proposition to become a legal reality.

In late January 1994, Adeline, the twins and I made a trip to the Canadian embassy in Portugal for our immigration interview. The Canadian embassy in South Africa could not process our application due to their quota being full for that year, so our immigration lawyer made arrangements for the embassy in Portugal to do the interview and process the application. From Portugal, the boys flew back home; but Adeline and I decided to pay our new country of choice a visit, with the hope of finding the ideal place to settle. The lawyer had set up our application to the Canadian Authorities for the purchase of a business in a fast-growing, West Coast city in British Columbia, but we also qualified to look for employment instead if we so chose. We eventually chose the city of Penticton in British Columbia as a place to purchase a business, and I made a deposit of funds into a safety deposit box at a local bank there. For good measure, and to ensure that this city posed as the best choice for us, we took a trip across to Toronto, where we stayed with friends of friends. Our visit coincided with a freeze-up of conditions, and we experienced the first real taste of a Canadian winter, an experience which confirmed the first venue on the West Coast as a good choice. We then flew back to our home country.

South Africa negotiated the elections for a new government in April 1994 and the ANC, with Nelson Mandela as the newly elected president, came into power. The peaceful transition surprised almost everyone—a testimony to the faith placed in God, and Mandela's vision for the country. Not much changed in our day-to-day lives, but I felt the tide would make a slow turn, and my prognosis of the future did not change. We all gained confidence in Mandela's leadership, but his age placed a limit on his ability to remain for the time it would take for a prosperous dispensation to take hold. In May 1994, Ray, Janet, and a family from Pastor Derek's church, a couple whom we knew well, left South Africa for Canada. Our application took a little longer, but in October 1994, we said goodbye to everyone. Many of the church members took the trip to the airport to see us off, a tearful separation for all of us. My brother Robert and sister-in-law, Eleanore, were also there; it would be six long years before we would see them again. My last impressions of my home country, viewed from the window seat of the Boeing 747 as it took off for Heathrow, London, provided an indelible memory of the land I grew up in. I felt my heart flutter at the thought that the place of my birth would soon become a distant memory.

In the interim, before our actual immigration, we decided that the geographic region in which our chosen destination lay came across as a little too arid for our liking. The larger city on Vancouver Island, originally chosen by our lawyer for a proposed business venture, appealed more to us. Ray, Janet, and their friends raved about this city, and both couples decided to call it their new home. They enjoyed a five-month advantage in research options, so we decided to take their word for it. My desire to start a future new church outreach still occupied my thoughts but I determined that the flow of events would dictate the possibility.

A day later we arrived at the airport in Vancouver, tired and travel-weary, to be met by Ray and Janet, who offered to pick us up and ferry us to the Island. We bunked with them for three nights before moving on to stay with one of our South African contacts, also resident in the city. The lady of the house, a South African immigrant and married to a Canadian gentleman who ran a construction company, invited us into their home with open arms. Three weeks later, we moved out of our temporary

The Bigger Picture

dwelling into a rental, and awaited the arrival of the container with all our possessions.

I didn't know it then, but my greatest trials still lay ahead.

23: My Greatest Mistake

We researched dozens of business opportunities in the weeks that followed our arrival in Canada and undertook visits to several of the realty companies in our new city of residence.

With the internet in its infancy foot-slogging and telephone calls became the means to narrow down the type of opportunity we thought would suit us best. I had it in mind to buy a business that would provide employment for the family; an enterprise that could support all of us and serve as a transition to whatever careers the boys might choose for themselves. In the interim, the twins managed to get part-time work as servers in a restaurant called The Pantry, a business owned by a South African immigrant with whom we later became friends. While working at this restaurant, Paul met the girl who six months later, became his wife.

The Pantry served as a meeting place for a cross-section of the city's inhabitants and on one particular evening, while our son Paul worked the evening shift, an immigrant family from New Zealand came for dinner. The family, a young woman with her parents, heard Paul's South African accent and enquired about his country of origin. After the meal, they invited him to visit and bring his parents along, as they wanted to meet us. I'm not sure if the invite stemmed from the attraction the young woman felt for Paul, or whether the parents wanted to be hospitable, but we felt it a noble gesture on their behalf. Paul, however, with his eyes on a coworker didn't share the same attraction for this young girl, but he accepted the invitation to get us hooked up with the family, and we paid them a visit. Adeline and I hit it off with Robert and Jill, the girl's parents, and we became household friends.

I shared our desire to purchase a business in which the family could find employment and Jill told us of a viable restaurant she thought might still be for sale in the city's largest shopping mall. The idea snared my interest so we visited the listing realtor. The realtor informed us that after the purchase of the business the owner left his home province of Quebec and moved to the West Coast to run it but his wife missed her family so much that they decided to instal a manager and move back home. Our realtor, a Christian brother, contacted the couple to see if they still wanted to sell. The owner told him he would consider a sale in the new year. I didn't know at the time that they wanted to reel in December's income to inflate their annual turnover.

In January 1995, I received a call from the realtor to ask if we were still interested in the purchase. In order to test the waters, I asked the realtor to put in an offer for half the asking price, in the hope they would at least counter; but he said he couldn't insult the owners with such a low offer. After Adeline and I discussed the matter, we decided to purchase the business at the asking price, provided the owner would carry a loan for half the amount, as we did not have enough money. They accepted and we signed the contract at the franchise office in Vancouver—my greatest mistake, and the worst decision I have ever made.

The twins, Adeline, and I went for two days' training at one of the franchise restaurants in Vancouver where for the first time an opportunity arose for me to discuss some of the hidden costs of doing business. After a revision of actual cost percentages I realized we would not be able to reduce the food costs, as hoped. No one revealed that the pre-December balance sheet figures (shown to me by the realtor) did not provide a true reflection of the business dynamics in the Mall. Unbeknown to us a large food chain that served as one of the major anchors vacated the mall in mid 1994 and a new anchor snatched up the space. This may not seem to be a huge change, but it affected the mall dynamics to quite an extent. In some unforeseen way, the change of anchors lessened the traffic flow of people who stayed for lunch during the week. Weekends in the food court remained steady, but weekdays became slim pickings. I originally viewed the balance sheets for the previous three years, which reflected good incomes for those periods, except that the 1994 income dropped off toward the end of that year. The franchise cited the Canadian economy as the problem for this drop, and they felt confident that the country would soon recover from its financial woes.

After the first day of training at the Vancouver store, I retired with Adeline to our hotel in a morbid state. I told her we had made a huge mistake in the purchase of the business, and should never have signed the contract. Had I known the law, or been privy to someone who did, I might have saved many future years of turmoil. The law allows for a seven-day "buyer's remorse" after the signing of any contract. I would only have lost the ten thousand dollar deposit. We persevered, however, and continued with the training. After two weeks of business, I began to feel a little better about the future. Paul joined us in the endeavor, and after two months his girlfriend joined us as well. They made all the different types of sandwiches and dealt with the customers while I worked the cash register and Adeline ran the kitchen. The first two weeks of operation spanned the school year's Spring Break, and many people visited the mall over that time. We maintained a busy workload for the break's ten-day period but due to the learning process many mistakes hampered the otherwise smooth transition.

Ray's wife, Janet, joined us as a helper and she soon proved herself to be a valuable asset. We employed four other young girls as servers and sandwich makers, plus we received help from an experienced franchise employee who helped with the initial set-up.

The food court vendors started the day at 6:00 am in order to be ready for the daily influx of customers at 8:30. In those early days of spring, we arrived in the dark and left in the dark at the end of the day. It took some getting used to, and I did not take well to the early-morning wake-up. Our income did not meet prior standards, and while I paid everyone else I could not pay Adeline or myself. We lived off the restaurant as much as possible, but our expenses merely contributed to the negative costs of the business. The franchise fees fell into arrears, and I stopped payment of them altogether, as we gained no benefit from the franchisor.

I soon stopped payments on the loan to our largest creditor, the previous owner of the business, there being little he could do about it at the time. He certainly did not want to take the business back, because he knew about the change in anchor dynamics and it would mean the provision of more money to keep the business afloat. We limped along without hope of redemption, other than to try and sell.

In early 1996, the mall manager approached me with a plan. He proposed we give off fifty percent of our space to a new vendor in the hope that the lower rent would hasten our financial salvation. Adeline and I agreed, as it seemed the only viable possibility for us. Renovations to accommodate the new venture, a concept called "The Weigh", took several weeks to complete and we offered up our tables and chairs to serve both businesses.

The Bigger Picture

The renovations, however, dampened the patronage of both businesses, and we had to work around each other in order to provide our relevant services.

The construction took six weeks to complete before both businesses could operate at full capacity. Our income suffered over this period, and with a new business in the same general space, we lost a certain amount of our old customers, who wanted to try the new concept. These circumstances lasted for about three months, and by the time I began to realize a small benefit from the rent reduction, our back rent had become a formidable debt for us to service.

We did our best, but with the scales tipped against us from the outset, financial parity became a lost cause. On my birthday in September 1996, the mall manager paid me an unexpected visit with a mandate to shut our business down. He made a generous offer; we could return on the following evening, after mall hours, and remove any equipment we wanted to keep. The rest would be auctioned off to pay the back rent.

I felt abandoned by the God whom I loved and served for so many years. I asked myself: how could this have happened? I faced bankruptcy for the first time in my life and, at the age of fifty-two years, there appeared little hope of any financial salvation.

At first, I remained confident that God would perform some sort of miracle to deliver us from this bondage. Much later, however, and with a certain amount of hindsight, I managed to make some sense of the whole affair. The fault lay with me—too little due diligence and blind trust in God. These two factors served to negate my clear view of the purchase details. On the day the manager shut us down, I sent the staff home with their mandatory lay-off pay and left Adeline and Paul to close up shop. After the short walk home I stopped in at the apartment block foyer to open our mailbox and found a sealed envelope—a note from the lawyer who facilitated the original registration of the business. The letter contained an invoice for the bi-annual registration of directors, an amount of two hundred and twenty-five dollars. Yeah, right! I thought. Due to the shock of the business loss and everything we owned it is difficult to describe my state of mind at the time. Another problem arose with our new apartment, purchased twelve months prior; it would now be lost to our creditors. Not only did we lose our business, but our home and all our money as well. I cannot even begin to describe the devastation I felt; my life appeared to be at an end, and my memories of all the ministry successes achieved in the past with New Beginnings Church and the school became hazy figments of the distant past. In contemplation of the precarious future I questioned the decision to leave my home country and wondered what we would have to do to survive.

The Bigger Picture

I picked up the phone to call the lawyer. I needed to explain why his bill could not be paid.

24: God's Response to Our Dilemmas

The question I want to raise at this point in my life's story is, how does God respond to our dilemmas when we ask for help? Does the God of the Bible overturn adverse circumstances to the advantage of his creation? I want to be clear on my perspective of the Creator's involvement in our daily lives on a real-time basis. When it comes down to the question of God's response to the prayers of His subjects, the real answer remains a matter of one's personal perspective and belief. I do feel, however, that the writers of both Testaments allowed their strong desires to portray a loving and protective deity who aids His children to influence their own perspectives. Because we have grown up in families with fathers and mothers who loved and cared for us, we believe that God's relationship is one as a parent to his children. We are made in God's image, therefore a belief that God will father us like an earthly parent would his child, is a reasonable deduction. No child can circumvent the basic need for nurture and sustenance. Families are seen as the backbone of society and the vehicle by which children can learn the skills that help them grow up into responsible contributors to society.

The Bigger Picture

Not apparent in this projection of God's fatherly role is the application of His "real time" action in response to the adverse circumstances often experienced by humankind. Does the Creator intervene as a result of our prayers? Does God change the order of things to accommodate a reversal of what may be a disastrous outcome, based on a decision we have made or that has been made on our behalf? Does God really help the sportsperson make good on a victory because of prayer? Which soldier in a war escapes the bullet when they both ask for protection as they fire upon each other? Why are many prayers not answered, or answered in the manner we would expect from a humane father? I know we have notions that suggest God sometimes answers in the negative, or God had another plan in mind, or God will provide a means of escape, but are these really the expectations we should have? Which one of us, as a parent, would not do everything in our power to protect our own? And yet we as humans do not have any form of omnipotence to perform miracles to protect our children. When things go wrong for our kids, we move mountains to protect them; but it would seem the God of the Bible has enthusiasm for only a limited number of miracles. Every such situation that requires the Creator's assistance is dowsed in prayer, but only a percentage are taken care of. Does the problem lie with the relationship, or with the prayer?

Maybe we have misconstrued the fundamentals of this relationship; could the reason behind this misdirected perspective be the desperate need humans have to feel safe? With all the apparent uncertainties in life do spiritually minded people desire a benevolence that demands complete protection and peace of mind? I suggest that God's role as a father is a metaphoric one; that the analogy does not extend into our real-life material situations, because God is a Spirit and we are flesh. Am I saying that the Creator does not care about us while the worst of things befall us? On the contrary. I believe that the Creator plays an immanent role in the creation, and has taken every care to provide the very best for all of us by means of allowing free will and personal decision-making. This is what I see as being a just and viable outworking of God's plan for all beings who have the capacity for sentient thought: the law of probability.[26] The law of probability is woven into every aspect of spacetime, and whatever decision we make will provide one of the infinite possibilities as an outcome. In other words, your decisions determine your outcomes, and provide the reality assigned to whatever that outcome brings. My purchase of a bad business was not due to the fact that other people pulled the wool over my eyes, but rather because I failed to do the due diligence required to reveal the negatives. I bypassed the need to do such deep research because I trusted God to protect my interests; but God never planned to step in and rescue me from my own bad choice, and my decision to purchase carried a consequence.

The Bigger Picture

God did, however, provide me with common sense to make good decisions—but it takes due diligence to work out what common sense is, and to make the right call. It's not that we don't put our trust in God for the outcome, but this form of trust should be invested in the provision already made before time began, the provision that good outcomes follow good decisions. This viewpoint accommodates the exercise of free will.

Although in general terms the theory of probability is based on 50% of a good or bad outcome, I would hesitate to ascribe this to life itself. In my experience life appears to offer more numerous negative outcomes than positive ones, so it is paramount that our children be taught the practice of accurate and diligent research. We should teach them to trust in the provision the Creator has already made in the decision-making process, and not to indulge in blind trust for the best outcome.

There are instances when we are unable to perform the necessary research for better outcomes, and will in these cases be forced to accept what ever probability spacetime assigns to our decisions. This is why we must take the good with the bad in life. My decision to purchase the soup-and-sandwich business yielded an important lesson about lack of observation. A more diligent scrutiny of the equipment in the restaurant would have revealed its breakdown potential due to age. Another problem lay in the high rent required by the landlords. I should have researched the dynamics of the mall with its change in business anchors, plus studied the drop off in income for the last half of the previous year before we made the purchase. Instead, I chose to ignore these signs, because I believed God had my back. After all, I (up to the time of the purchase) lived as a committed Christian and contributor to the cause for more than twenty-three years. This remained an undefined thought in the back of my mind, one to which I never gave any substance or voice.

One caveat with regard to the above perspective requires a mention here: It may be construed that I have suggested a disconnect between God and the minds of humankind; that there is no influence by the Spirit on the decisions we make. But this is not true. Scripture reveals the essence of the "incarnate dwelling" of the human soul by God; and in this incarnation, one would expect a transfer of thought to the one indwelled. I believe this to be an astute deduction that deserves qualification. The difficulty with the transfer of thought or information from Spirit to flesh is the free-will factor that operates through the human intellect and emotions. As mentioned in a previous chapter, the writers of the Testaments did not receive verbatim dictation, but the kernels of ideas that they interpreted through the veil of human experience. The people who managed this transfer better than most were the mystics, proponents of a type of meditation that allowed the human senses and the mind, the entity we call the "lower self," to be aligned with the "higher self," the part of your consciousness that is the Creator.

The Bigger Picture

The lower self is the part of consciousness considered human, and reflects personality, intellect, emotions and free will. It is the "you" that interacts with the world. The higher self is that part of consciousness where your lower self and God interact. Both the lower and higher selves are you, and both are God. Your lower self is where you have the governing influence, and the higher self is where the Creator has the governing influence. Both selves are of the same stream of consciousness; and in this way, it has been said that God is living through you to experience the created universe. The dual perception of you as being separate from God is merely an illusion created by the lower self for the purpose of interaction with the material world.

Learning to meditate like the great mystics of the past did, and like those extant today are still doing, will bring your lower self into a closer association with your higher consciousness. This is how we can better interpret the spiritual concepts the Spirit would have us learn for making better decisions in life. It is unfortunate that the art of meditation has been largely lost to the Western Christian world, because it has been seen as an Eastern practice and vilified as devilish. The devil is not a real "person," but Christian fundamental propaganda and dogma would have everyone believe that if one meditates, the mind will inadvertently be invaded by bad spirits. The truth about mediation is that it relaxes the meditator and aids focus on the higher self, where God's influence on the human mind is greatest.

Colin Setterfield

It is said that there is strength in numbers. We know this to be true, and the writers of the New Testament cottoned onto this and included a warning in the scripture: "...neglect not the gathering of yourselves together as you see the day drawing near..." This statement emphasizes there is strength and protection in numbers, a fact we cannot deny; but its truth is subjective, because it works both for the conservation of vital information and the converse of protection against disinformation. The writers of scripture knew that people, in general, are gullible to disinformation, and that if they opened their minds to other voices in the world, they might easily be led astray. They were doing their best to protect their ideals. I have experienced the practices of a closed group that attempts to keep the blinders on its patrons in the form of the vilification of anything outside the group's accepted parameters or doctrines. It's not that the information contained in ancient scripture is wrong, but rather a misguided attempt by humanity to interpret reality.

Several years later, I would discern that my religious blinkers hampered my eventual discovery of the bigger picture. In the next chapter, I will pick up again on that fateful day when Adeline and I lost our business, and the subsequent course of events.

25: Some Unexpected Help

I picked up the phone, keyed in the attorney's phone number, and waited. My emotions ran high, a warning sign of a borderline combative attitude. The secretary connected me with Louis Plazzer, the lawyer responsible for the set up of the business registration details.

"I have received your bill for director's registration," I told him, "but I have some bad news."

"What's happened?" he asked.

I hesitated, took a deep breath and answered. "Our business has been closed down by the mall. Despite sharing our area with The Weigh, we are not making ends meet and I am into a back rent situation. The mall manager decided that we will not be able to recover, so he stepped in. I will try to pay your bill once we've determined where we stand financially, but it doesn't look promising."

The lawyer's comment came after a brief silence. "I'm terribly sorry to hear that. What are you doing after five p.m. this afternoon?" he asked.

"I don't have any plans," I said.

"You must be feeling a bit shattered and helpless at the moment. Please, won't you and your wife come down to my office? I want to advise you on what to do next."

He appeared genuine about his offer. "I don't have any money to pay you for your service," I said.

"Payment won't be necessary. I am prepared to help on a pro-bono basis."

I breathed a sigh of relief. "Thank you. Adeline and I will be there a few minutes after five."

I replaced the phone on the receiver and stared out of the window at the tall trees on the sports ground complex across the road. The appearance of a ray of light on the other end of my dark tunnel brought a small measure of comfort. After Adeline arrived home we huddled together on the couch, both in contemplation of the course ahead of us. My son Paul and his young wife, now both out of work, arrived at 4:30 p.m. For them, however, the ordeal would have less impact due to their eligibility for unemployment insurance. As directors Adeline and I did not qualify for this safety net, so we needed to find other means of support as soon as possible. The apartment's mortgage, plus strata fee and our car payment, all hung like dark clouds over our future. We also owed a huge amount of money on the business, and I our largest supplier still awaited payment for its latest delivery of supplies. I cried out to the God of the Bible for

The Bigger Picture

help; I knew all the scriptural theory of the Savior's love, but a notion of abandonment flooded my soul.

Shortly after five p.m. that afternoon, Adeline and I arrived at the lawyer's offices. The secretary asked us to wait while Mr. Plazzer completed a phone conversation; a few minutes later, he called us in and offered us a seat. "I want to tell you how sorry I am that this has befallen you," he said sympathetically. "You must both be feeling depressed and helpless,"

The many times that I provided counsel for couples, or those who suffered a loss of some kind, came to mind; and I realized the irony of my situation.

"We don't know what to do next," I admitted. "I have never been in such a predicament. We've only been in the country for two years, and now this."

Louis came up with some valuable advice. "I want you to take the mall manager up on the offer of removing anything of value. Ask a friend if you can store the stuff in their garage; if no one can help you, I will make a plan to make some space in one of my garages. I have a large property on the outskirts of town, but you will need to arrange for the transport. I also want you to go to a different bank from the one you use for your business and private accounts. Open a safety deposit box, and whatever money you have, draw it out of the current accounts and store it in the box."

"What will we do to stay alive?" I asked.

"You'll both have to try and find jobs, but in the interim, try to set up some private sales on whatever equipment you're able to get out of the restaurant."

"What about the mortgage and strata fees for the apartment?" asked Adeline.

The lawyer leaned back in his chair. "Stop paying all your current accounts, no matter what they are. I promise you I will keep you in your apartment for as long as possible. We will send your largest creditor, the previous business owner, a letter and explain that you are prepared to pay him the bankruptcy fee, normally about two thousand dollars, in lieu of an application for court protection, and we will see what he wants to do about it. You have no assets that he can take, so he'll know it won't help to sue you. The apartment's mortgage will go into default. Since you are a first-time buyer in Canada, CMHC will take care of the bank loan."

"Won't they kick us out of the apartment when we stop payment?" I asked.

"Don't worry about a thing. The law will not allow them to put you on the street with immediate effect. The mortgage holder will try to set up a forced sale of the premises, but these things take time. If you are forced into bankruptcy, there are rules to protect income under seventeen hundred dollars a month. You will also be allowed to keep a home and a car, which have a minimum equity below a certain amount. You are going to be okay. Get used to working everything on a cash basis, and use the safety deposit box as you would a regular bank account."

I felt a measure of emotional relief at the lawyer's words. "I feel bad for my creditors. It was never my intention to do anyone out of money," I said.

He flashed me a benevolent smile. "Don't feel sorry for them. They're business people, and everyone knows that all business is a risk. Eventually, everyone moves on, so this is a time you should be taking care of yourselves."

We left the lawyer's office in a better frame of mind. I still felt like a murderer on death row, but my estimation of the legal fraternity had gone up by leaps and bounds. I contacted a friend who had been a member of our church in South Africa and asked if we could borrow his cube van to remove the larger items from the restaurant. We took the large fridge and freezer, the cooler, the electric meat slicer, and certain items of crockery and cutlery. Our New Zealand friends offered the basement of their home as a storage area for all the removed items. We sold the large items, and whatever could not be sold was given away to the Salvation Army thrift store. The sales did not net a large amount of money, but at least we could put food on the table for a while.

The realtor who sold us the apartment also lived in the same block. His position as chairman of the strata committee meant he would know how the committee dealt with defaulters, and I decided to tell him about our problem. His sympathetic attitude surprised me. We discussed the country's bad economic period and he told me that several hundred businesses per day faced bankruptcy due to the bad economic environment. He suggested I sit tight and wait for the mortgage provider to contact us. I asked what he thought might happen with the second mortgage carried by the Chinese couple, the original owners of the apartment.

"You will be surprised! I believe they will most likely walk away," he said. "It is something nascent in their culture, and I have experienced this a few times when deals with them have gone bad."

"They probably believe in karma," I said.

The realtor was right in his assumption. The Chinese couple walked away. I never received a lawyer's letter from them, or any threat of legal action. I marveled at such composure, and could not respect their view on life more. One evening I received a call from our largest creditor, the owner of the business, who refused the one-off payment in lieu of the potential bankruptcy, and insisted we still owed him over eighty-thousand dollars. My answer to his dilemma summed up the situation in a matter-of-fact manner.

The Bigger Picture

"How would you like to be in my shoes? I am fifty-two years old, and the prospects of getting a job in this economic climate are extremely grave. We both need to accept the status quo and assume the risks of being in business. I have lost everything, and to recover from this situation will take a miracle."

He couldn't argue with my reasoning, but expressed the view that he would like to keep an eye on any future progress I might make and recover as much of the debt as possible. I told him that if he was thinking of suing me, I would go bankrupt, and we left it at that. Louis Plazzer kept up a correspondence with him with regard to possible options; at one point, he offered to reduce the debt to twenty-five thousand dollars, and asked if I would be prepared to consider paying it off over a period of time. My lawyer refused.

Adeline managed to get a position with a local vet as a receptionist, while I continued to apply for work through news ads and the local job agencies. Ray, in the meantime, came to my rescue. Getting a job was not as difficult for him due to his younger age, and after an offer to go into business came his way, he asked if I might like to apply for his current job. I did so and got the position, which paid a salary plus a car allowance, and things started to look up for us. I opened a new bank account for the deposit of the income each month, but always immediately withdrew the money in cash for deposit into the safety deposit box as Louis had instructed me to do.

Six months later, we heard from the apartment's mortgage provider, a large insurance and loans company. Adeline answered the call and a lady representative enquired as to our wellbeing.

"We notice you have not paid your mortgage for the last six months. What has happened?"

Adeline told her about the demise of our business and she responded with empathy. "I'm terribly sorry this happened to you, Mrs. Setterfield. Don't you worry about a thing; you and your husband should just carry on with your lives and sit tight."

I couldn't believe their benevolent attitude toward our default on the mortgage. We accepted it as God's provision and carried on with our lives. Two years later we heard from the mortgage provider again, the same lady as before.

"We are sending a realtor around to view the apartment. It will be sold as soon as a buyer can be found," she said.

By this time our joint employment income and the small amount of cash in the safety deposit box became our lifeline to survival. The only regular payment I continued to make throughout the initial period of insolvency was the car, our only form of transport. Another financial blow, however, dampened our ardor: my employer, after a full year of competition with a host of newer business arrivals, decided to service the Island from the mainland and closed the local office. This meant retrenchment for me; and for the first time, I went onto employment insurance. A year later, I managed to get a job selling insurance and mutual funds with North West Life, a large insurance conglomerate based in Vancouver. In July 1999, the realtor appointed to sell our apartment, advised us of a possible sale and offered some good advice.

"When the new buyer contacts you, tell him that the appliances are not included in the sale, and that he will have to purchase them from you."

I thought this might be a ruse to put the buyer off and thereby keep Adeline and I in the apartment for a longer period. Not long after the realtor's call, the purchaser a local businessman, made contact with me. I broached the subject of the appliances with the expectation he would walk away from the deal but he did not flinch. He said if we wanted to continue to live in the apartment for a while, it would be helpful to him, as his daughter, for whom he made the purchase, could not take occupation for at least another six months. He set up a very reasonable payment for me, and said that the cost of the appliances could be taken off the rent. The arrangement suited Adeline and I well, as we needed to find a new place to live, and this gave us the time to do just that.

In December 1999, we decided to make an effort to purchase a new home. We needed to test the waters despite a measure of skepticism, to see if it might be possible to qualify for another mortgage. A surprise awaited us.

26: Dodging a Bullet

Adeline and I waited in the broker's office for a life-changing phone call from a prospective mortgage provider. I felt sure we would be turned down. Our broker, a friendly and empathetic person, took in the details about the business failure and consequential default on the apartment's mortgage. For almost three years we heard nothing further about outstanding debt. I know our lawyer shared some hard facts with the seller of the business about certain non-disclosures. He posited that a counter-lawsuit might be brought against the franchise and the seller due to the non-disclosure of vital information with regard to the true state of all the kitchen equipment, much of which needed to be replaced in the months that followed the purchase. The lawyer also made a point about the inflated price of the sale which did not reflect the real value of the business at the time. In the end, we dodged the bankruptcy bullet because the seller elected to absorb the loss and not to sue.

The phone interrupted our small talk. The broker answered, listened to what the mortgage provider had to say, then replaced the phone on its receiver and frowned.

"Are you sure your mortgage was backed by CMHC?" he asked.

"I'm positive. We had been in the country for less than a year when we applied, so we were first-time buyers. I remember seeing it on the paperwork," I said.

"That's really strange. The representative says he can't find your names anywhere in the system."

Adeline and I exchanged glances. "Does that mean they'll back a mortgage for us?" she asked.

The broker nodded. "The representative said that as far as he could tell, there was nothing to stop us from making the application. Do you have a home in mind you would like to purchase?"

A mobile home park in the north end of our city offered several used homes for sale and one particular unit, a deceased estate, suited our exact need. Mobile homes cost a lot less than conventional ones; you did not buy the land, but rented it for a fee. This meant we could purchase one of these units with a small deposit and pay an affordable monthly pad rental. I knew we could make an offer for less than the asking price. The seller, a surviving spouse, now lived in an old-age home and wanted to offload the unit as quickly as possible.

Half an hour later we walked out of the broker's office with the promise of a mortgage and hastened to the park to put in an offer. A month later, we moved into our new home.

The Bigger Picture

Christian fellowship continued to be the most important aspect of our daily lives. Ray and Janet found a charismatic church they liked and we started attending services on a regular basis. In due course the pastor asked me to help out with the preaching load and he appeared pleased to have the sudden inclusion of several new families. The pastor, a man in his forties suffered from diabetes and over a period of years lost both kidneys to the disease. A matching donor came to the rescue and for several years the pastor survived on a borrowed kidney. He never complained about his plight, which prompted us to give him every possible assistance in his ministry.

In 1997 the pastor made a decision to retire. He wanted to hand the ministry over to a younger man, and several of the congregation members felt he should rather ask me to consider the position. My credentials, renewed by a Canadian Christian ministerial organization, made me a viable prospect for the post, plus the congregation members enjoyed my sermons. It seemed like a good opportunity to step back into full-time ministry again; however, the pastor's wife carried some sort of bias against Adeline and I. To complicate my application the pastor had drawn close to Ray and wanted him to take over the reins. I have always believed that experience counts a great deal in any ministry, and Ray's thoughts centered more around the support of ministry, than the need to direct it. I knew Ray well, and agreed with his conclusion. I had always found him to be an astute business-minded person who possessed little patience for the vagaries of human nature.

Not too long after that, Ray and I both felt that the church would flounder with a pastor who refused to face certain realities, unable to take the full responsibility of leadership. He no longer appeared to have the ability, due to his illness, to make rational decisions. A member of the church association to whuch the pastor belonged visited one weekend and encouraged him to step down in favor of a more capable person, be it myself or someone from outside, but the pastor refused the counsel. Ray and I both came to the conclusion that our ministry, now passed its useful point of meaningful contribution in this particular church, would be better applied elsewhere.

To backtrack a little (before the demise of our business) I met the pastor of a church situated in Victoria, a larger city on the southern tip of the Island, who visited our city for the day and happened to stop in at our restaurant for lunch. Several years prior, while in oversight of the church's mission program, he journeyed to South Africa to be involved in a mission there. Due to the retirement of the pastor in the local home church, however, they called him back to take over the reins. While in South Africa, he started a group called Circuit Teaching International for the aid of rural country pastors not blessed with a formal bible education. CTI sent qualified ordained ministers to provide counsel and teaching for these shepherds on a short term basis.

I preached one morning under invitation at my colleague's church in Victoria, and a Christian brother approached me after the service to consider an involvement with CTI.

"All expenses are paid by the ministry, and you will stay in the homes of these pastors while in the foreign country chosen for the ministry", he said.

I conceded that the opportunity would be a welcome interlude and paid my first visit to Mexico in August 1997. This three-week stint of ministry turned out to be a wonderful experience and education in rural mission work. Before I left on my journey, Adeline and I, along with Janet and Ray, made a decision to search for a new spiritual home. In my absence Ray and Janet attended a Sunday meeting at a new church situated on the outskirts of our city and came away with a positive experience. On my return from the CTI mission to Mexico, Adeline and I paid a visit to this church to see if it might become a suitable spiritual home for us. Ray and I then met with the pastor of the old church, and after some lively conversation, we parted ways with him and his fellowship.

It did not take us long to fit into the new congregation, a group of enthusiastic young people, zealous for the Lord. Pastor Godfrey, after our initial acquaintance and induction as new members, involved me in some Sunday morning Bible studies and preaching opportunities for which I felt grateful.

The idea of full-time pastorship began to grow distant for me as I concentrated on my new job with North West Life. I sat the Level One insurance exam and passed it on the first try. My main portfolio of insurance catered to seniors and the elderly, to whom I sold funeral insurance. Pastor Godfrey shared some salient details with regard to his life and ministry; his prior involvement in a professional music group before he came to know the Lord, placed him in a unique position to lead the church's music and their rendition of gospel songs rivaled the quality of many professional groups in the music industry. One negative fact he shared about the establishment of the small local church stemmed from the attitude of his home church in North Vancouver. It would appear that Pastor Godfrey ruffled some egotistical feathers of the home church leadership by his decision to start a new work on the Island. The Vancouver based church leadership told him that the initiative to set such a vision in motion should have been theirs and not his. They would therefore not offer any financial support for the endeavor, nor would they take any responsibility for the new church's future. A tense relationship existed between Pastor Godfrey and the old apostle of the Vancouver church. They came to visit on occasions when asked to preach but never accepted the work as a legitimate church plant. The exchanges appeared a little strained and guarded, with a true prima donna performance put on by the old apostle.

I soon picked up on more differences in their doctrinal beliefs and got the impression that our inclusion into the Island fellowship came to be viewed with some suspicion by the main group. The old apostle invited Adeline and I to attend a meeting with him and his elders, to determine the veracity of our Christian faith. It would be a weekend I will not forget. I thought it respectful to agree to the interview; besides I had nothing to hide. On the Saturday of the weekend in question, we attended a group picnic on a soccer field in North Vancouver, where the entire church gathered for some recreational fellowship. That evening we met with the old apostle. Both Adeline and I felt we were under some sort of investigation as the old man dithered and fussed over things he felt were important to their members. We were exhorted to comply with all the church's beliefs, rules, and regulations, or we would be asked to leave. The old man prayed, spoke in tongues, and called upon the Holy Spirit to reveal any deviousness which we might unknowingly subscribe to. He repeated things already covered several times, and I had the distinct feeling he suffered an early form of dementia.

The Sunday morning meeting proved my theory to be correct, because the old man insisted he needed to preach the morning sermon (against the will of his son, the main assistant pastor). Midway through the sermon, no one understood the theme or the point of the talk which appeared to be aimed at the devil, and wolves in sheep's clothing; perhaps a subtle dig at Adeline and I. After an hour of aimless rants, gesticulation, spitting and sinner-bashing, his son ambled up behind him and took his arm to lead him away from the pulpit. We could hear his indignation as the assistant pastor led him down the steps, into a room behind the pulpit area. He may have been one of Vancouver's brightest in his younger days, but senility appeared to have set in. I felt embarrassed for him, but there was nothing anyone could do but understand the condition with empathy.

Over the next two years, I began to feel uncomfortable about some of the beliefs that this group advocated. My history of one-way-only fundamentalism, which I thought had been dealt with, started to get the better of me; and instead of accepting Pastor Godfrey's position on the doctrinal differences, I began to feel I didn't belong. Ray, on the other hand, did not seem to worry about it much, so I tried to shrug it off and get on with life. But one day, Ray came to me and began to confide certain reservations about the church. He mentioned details about a chance meeting with a couple, new to the Island, who wanted to reach out to other expatriates and get to know the people in general. The couple I shall call Brian and Patricia invited Ray and Janet to a barbecue on a Saturday night, and Ray felt it would be a good thing for us to get to know them. The invitation, Ray said, extended to any of his friends who wanted to come along.

The Bigger Picture

We attended the barbecue, and discovered that Brian and Patricia, both strong Christians with a mandate from their home church in South Africa, believed in God's call on their lives to start a new church on the Island. The organization they belonged to in South Africa, started by a converted martial arts celebrity, attracted a huge following with many established churches in different parts of the world, and I knew their doctrinal beliefs to be similar to my own.

We enjoyed a great time of fellowship at the barbecue, and when we left that evening, I prayed over Brian and Patricia—that their efforts in the establishment of a new church in the city would be successful.

Two days later, I received a phone call from Pastor Godfrey.

"Are you and Adeline looking for a new church? It came to my notice that you visited with another South African couple who want to start a new fellowship in the city."

I assured him that we entertained no such aspiration.

"We initially did not know of their mandate to start a church. You can relax; we are not looking for a new fellowship," I insisted.

It may seem ironic that these two pastors, Brian and Godfrey, later became good friends; but our resolve to remain with Pastor Godfrey's fellowship would come under more tension through an unexpected development.

27: Jumping Churches Again

In July 1999, Adeline and I discussed the implications of another change with regard to our home-based fellowship. Although I still felt a little uneasy about certain aspects of Pastor Godfrey's doctrinal beliefs, these did not constitute a solid reason to pull up the roots laid down as a member of his church. I remembered back to my days of full-time ministry and how the defections of church members saddened me. Our earlier decision to leave our sickly pastor and his church made me feel like a heartless deserter despite the apparent justifications. The obvious and qualified applicant to have taken over that ministry at the time would have been me, but the rejection of my experience and credentials, for what I considered to be less than feasible reasons, still haunted me. This brought back the memory of Pastor Derek's sudden change of vision for the Eternal Life Church in South Africa, a recollection that placed me once again in a struggle to keep the call of God alive in my heart.

I recalled how in those days of my full-time ministry people left the church for what appeared to be less than sufficient reasons; but now, with the shoe on the other foot, the experience scribed a full circle. The shepherd, who in the past felt the pain

The Bigger Picture

of the occasional desertion by one of the flock, now prepared himself to give one of those dubious reasons.

Adeline maintained that she could not identify with any of the lady members of Pastor Godfrey's church. She no longer enjoyed the worship or the sermons, and I sensed the build up of a resistance to spiritual matters. This admission from her shocked me to the core. When someone you love dearly tells you something is wrong, it makes you listen. I tried to put up reasons why this feeling of alienation bothered her, but in the end, I realized that as a couple we faced a crossroad. After all, a happy wife means a happy life.

Christians sometimes allude to the fact that there is no such thing as a coincidence, because all the aspects of life are a part of God's divine plan, an allusion which holds a measure of truth. This measure of truth, however, does not pertain to a sudden reaction to any "real time" event but exists as a preplanned probability woven into the spacetime continuum.

A few weeks prior to our discussion Adeline received an invitation to have tea with a group of ladies, all members of Pastor Brian's new church. One of the ladies, who knew us well from our first Canadian church experience, posited that the event did not constitute an official church meeting and that this ladies group met on a casual basis from time to time. Adeline accepted the invitation and attended on two occasions. She enjoyed the fellowship of these ladies who all identified with her dilemma.

I discovered that these women were more Adeline's age, and none of them indulged in super-spiritual talk, just ordinary housewives and mothers. The ladies at Pastor Godfrey's church were all much younger, and Adeline did not fit in with them. I understood why she wanted to leave; she had no friends. Although Ray and I got on extremely well despite his much younger age, Janet, even younger, made a close friendship with her difficult for Adeline.

I decided to be open with Pastor Godfrey about the status quo. We sat down together, discussed the matter and much to my surprise, he understood the problem. He said he would call Pastor Brian and discuss the possibility of Adeline and I joining their church. He maintained that it would be better for Adeline to be in a situation where she felt more comfortable, so that she could continue to grow in the Spirit.

A week later, we joined Pastor Brian. The fledgling church with about thirty members, a testament of the pastor's acumen, received us with open arms. Pastor Brian and Patricia used their home as a venue, but it became clear that a larger meeting place would soon be needed. Ray and Janet decided not to leave Pastor Godfrey, a decision I agreed with. I didn't want to be the reason for anyone else leaving his church. Ray and I had also grown a little distant over the time we fellowshipped with Pastor Godfrey, and I think that maybe we both felt we should begin to define our own spiritual futures. We remained friends, but for the next year we did not fellowship much together. Ray's new job with the local cable company, a fast-growing concern and destined to become the most prolific TV service provider in the country, took up much of his free time. I am grateful to Ray for the years he served as one of my elders in the ministry, and also as one of my closest friends. He introduced both my boys, Paul and Andrew, to the cable company, and arranged interviews for them.

We fellowshipped at Pastor Brian's church for about eight months. I preached several sermons over this time, but Pastor Brian's different style of ministry and the way he handled relationships, came across to me as heavy-handed. He did not fear confrontations with people who crossed him and although we got on well together, I recognized a different ministerial approach—one that I felt uncertain about. He once took Adeline to task for being too strict with her class in the Sunday school and not only scolded her for it, but removed her from the position. We grew up in an environment that advocated a good deal of child discipline, but it appeared a new and more liberal philosophy now ruled the roost. This move caused Adeline some stress, and she started to withdraw. Pastor Brian also said some hard things about Ray, who still fellowshipped in Pastor Godfrey's church at the time, and made no bones about the fact that he did not want Ray and Janet to follow me to his church. This came about when Ray and Janet unexpectedly arrived one Sunday evening. I have no idea what prompted Pastor Brian's comments, but I think they may have been as a result of something Pastor Godfrey said at one of our Pastor's prayer meetings.

I gathered that Ray and Janet no longer enjoyed a stress-free relationship with Pastor Godfrey. When an occasion presented itself I shared Pastor Brian's comments with Ray and suggested that it would not be a smart move for him and Janet to leave their present church to fellowship with us. I will, however, say this for Pastor Brian, he showed no concern over the loss of membership as most pastor's did and made sure that his agenda stayed afloat. This may seem to be an admirable quality (and perhaps it is), but I couldn't help think that a more tactful approach might have been required in his decisions. I will stand to be corrected on this if necessary, because over the years of my experience in ministry, we ministers tend to bend over backward to accommodate the people we serve. I am the first to admit that few of us find a good balance in this area of our priestly service.

In March 2000, we moved into our new mobile home in the north end of the city. After the purchase, Paul, Andrew, and I, with the help of a friend, refurbished the interior of the home. We took a credit line with the local Home Depot store to do all the work. To my surprise, Ray dropped by one morning and found me at home. At first, I thought he was curious to see our new place, but while we enjoyed a cup of coffee, he shared the real reason for his visit.

The Bigger Picture

"A small window of opportunity has arisen for us to start a new fellowship. We have three families who have left Godfrey's church and are looking for a new spiritual home. They asked about you; whether you might be willing to join us in the venture?"

Ray's words took me by surprise. My secular job of insurance sales required a great deal of effort and the thought of a return to full-time ministry, although attractive, lay dormant. I also attended seminars to keep my insurance education intact, and spent at least one full day at home phoning prospective clients. Although not the type of work I enjoyed, the sales brought us a steady income. Ray's statement intrigued me.

"Who are the families, and why did they leave the church?" I asked.

He named the families, all of whom I knew well, but he didn't give me the full story with regard to one of the couples. I found out much later that this couple, whom I will call Justin and Sheila Kendrick, experienced some marriage problems and felt Pastor Godfrey's counsel lacked matrimonial sense. While an astute minister of the gospel Pastor Godfrey lacked any formal ministerial training, perhaps the reason why the leaders of his home church in North Vancouver never accepted his pastorship. The Kendricks sought counsel from Ray, and he advised them with a greater measure of wisdom and advised them to find a new spiritual home. I detected a real change in Ray's attitude toward Pastor Godfrey and when I asked him about it he cited a lack of vision and experience on the young pastor's behalf.

Ray continued. "You had tremendous vision and leadership ability when you pastored in South Africa. You built a great work in New Beginnings Church, and I don't doubt you can do it again."

I believe I felt the Spirit prompt me to consider the possibility. Almost all new, modern churches are born out of splits and fallouts between members. I thought back on my extensive experiences in South Africa, and Canada appeared to be no different. Fallouts between leaders and congregation members appeared to be common amongst the Pentecostal churches on the Island. The phenomenon, not restricted to these "Spirit-filled" denominations, also manifested in some of the mainline churches. A few weeks prior to our move from Pastor Godfrey's church one of the long-standing main-line congregations in our city suffered a problem that turned into a nasty split. That old demon of crisis appeared to haunt most of the new church establishments after a certain period of elapsed time. A study I once did in college showed that congregants pass through a three-year honeymoon period of euphoric excitement and discovery after a church's initial establishment. After that, a certain amount of polarization starts, and people begin to focus on what they don't like about each other.

The Bigger Picture

Ray's kind words of encouragement fell into fertile soil: to establish new churches and grow them into viable fellowships appeared to be my calling. As I look back on this meeting with Ray, I realize, more than ever, that the mind (and faith) can make you believe anything is true. I felt an excitement and a new lease on life that lifted me out of the failure of the past business experience, and I couldn't wait to share the idea with Adeline when she returned home from work. Ray left after I told him I would consider an involvement in the venture.

What I didn't know at the time would soon become painfully evident to me. The couple with the marriage problem, the Kendricks, fellowshipped in by-gone years at one of the aforementioned Pentecostal churches before a major split forced the pastor to leave the Island. The Kendricks, bonded to this pastor, saw a potential with our new venture to establish a work to which their old pastor friend could return and assume the leadership role. I'm not sure if Ray made it clear to them that I would be the best candidate to lead the new congregation, but it seems they might have been under the false assumption that there would be no official leader to start with, and that we would all pitch in to establish the work. Had I known this one fact, I might have declined Ray's invitation of any involvement.

Colin Setterfield

28: Divine Inspiration?

Everyone is born into this world for a purpose; one that is never quite evident to us. We begin to understand that without relationships no one can experience the real meaning of life. It starts with a mother's love and the bonding process with both parents—if we are fortunate enough to have them, which most of us do. Our parents become the important first role models, but this begins to change as we develop minds of our own. After we assume some form of control over our lives, the world becomes an exciting but more dangerous place.

The first encounter with spiritual concepts comes to each of us early in life, manifested in the form of questions about the natural world with its water, earth, mountains, seas, and the stars in the night sky. I believe these discoveries spark the very first spiritual experience most of us have as children. This appeared to be true for me, but perhaps not everyone questions these things in the same way. The point I make here is that we all experience a subtle nudge toward the infinite through the mystery of our surroundings. Religion teaches us there is a God who created everything, but there are many who do not agree that this is so. Church life may be an early experience for us due to our parent's association with a religion. As children, we may have been forced to take part in the ecclesiastical scene, or we may have seen the church as a place where people meet, hear a sermon, and discuss things of apparent importance.

My agnostic parents never attended church, so for me as a child, spirituality did not play an important part in daily life. I think I saw the church as a place where people with real problems went, a sort of hospital for the mentally wounded. Children seldom connect the church with a spiritual learning experience; they see Sunday School as an extension of normal school, with its propensity for memory education and discipline. It is later on, as the children grow up to become teenagers, that some form of spiritual understanding develops, but all too often life itself intervenes and draws them away. The bright lights of the world provide exciting possibilities for young impressionable minds and religion, if pondered at all, is merely another ruse that adults use to prevent stimulating experiences. Older teens, together with young adults, become more open to the concept of religion when they experience the pressures of the modern world. The big questions of where we came from, why we are here, and what our final destination will be, appear to assert a greater pressure when we start the search for the greater purpose of our existence.

Religion is based on ancient scriptures and texts that tell the stories of peoples' relationship with the one infinite God (or gods) that created all things. The events inherent in these stories have all taken place in the distant past, times to which the modern seeker struggles to relate. It is, therefore, necessary to look beyond the ancient living conditions, modes of transport, and cultural differences that underpin the original stories in order to extract real meaning. Human nature throughout history has not changed much, if at all, so the spiritual concepts, although penned in ancient times, will still reflect on the problems of human nature. Love, fear, hate, anger, and prejudice are as present today as they have ever been.

There are many poignant truths to be uncovered in the Bible but before anyone accepts scripture as the "inspired work" of the Creator there are two aspects to be considered.

The first aspect to be taken into account is an allusion to the direct inspiration of texts. I will give one example. The Bible's four Gospels, written many years after the original incidents occurred, have, with the time-lapse between actual events and the penned words, suffered a discontinuity of formal record. This may have contributed to the errors and differences between the authors' writings. Mark, the first Gospel to be written appeared around 70 CE, some forty years after the crucifixion. In the case of Matthew and Luke, the works, written as late as 80 CE, suffer an even greater lapse of time between the main event and the record; and that of John's record, written around 100 CE. There is no positive proof of the presence of the authors at the crucifixion. Most theologians believe the reference to the "beloved disciple" in John's Gospel is a reference to John's presence, (the disciple that Jesus loved), but this is speculative.

The many differences in the details of each gospel are not only a matter of personal perception, but they are an indication God did not directly inspire the knowledge. It is more probable that the stories passed down by the actual eyewitnesses, provided the source of the inspiration that led to the eventual written records.

Another fact that adds to the mystery: the Gospel authors have assumed names given to them by the religious academic authorities of long ago. It is apparent that at least two of the writers were Hebrews who intended to create a narrative that still projected the Jewishness of their religion, and highlighted the transformative power of God through a Jewish rabbi named Jesus. At no time in their writings do they reject their Hebrew roots or announce a new religion. They also proclaimed the universal love of God for all His creatures and benefits of salvation to be awarded to the "who so ever".

So: what does this mean for seekers who want to apply scriptural principles as foundational truths in their own lives? It suggests a reliance on the memories of the eyewitness accounts passed down to younger scribes who, fifty years later or more, decided to make records of the stories for posterity's sake. Our problem, as Christians, is that we become predisposed to overlook all possible anomalies in scripture because we want to believe that the record is perfect. The Apostle Paul writes to Timothy and lays the foundation for this belief through the exhortation that "all scripture is given by inspiration of God and is profitable for doctrine, reproof, for correction, for instruction in righteousness." 2 Tim 3;16. By "all scripture", Paul referred to the main legal compendium of scripture used in the synagogues of the time, (the Greek Septuagint).[27] The rabbis also used the Talmud, a central text of Rabbinic Judaism, and the Midrash, a genre of rabbinic literature, interpretations, and commentaries. Because of his legal background, the contents of these texts would have been gospel to Paul—foundational to his belief as a Pharisee.[28] It is little wonder that he exhorted Timothy to accept these scriptures as the direct, inspired work of God.

It is a general consensus by fundamentalists that the authors penned what God told them to, and wrote when God directed them. This view, however, does not gel with the concept of free will or the process of personal discovery of "seek and ye shall find". It is also suspicious that God would make a sudden decision to have things recorded some fifty years after the fact. The dogmatic inclusion by the Catholic Church of the New Testament writings as "inspired" works, came more than 330 years after the first circulation of the epistles. More inclusions/exclusions made by the Second Council of Trullan in 692, the 39 Articles of 1563, the Council of Trent in 1545, and the Westminster

Council in 1647, further reveal how the scriptures became the subject of change.

I suggest that the entire matter of what became scripture was left to men who made important decisions of thier inclusion in the general canon of scripture and happened after times of great debate, tension, and ambitious posturing by the religious authorities of the times.

The second aspect a seeker should take into account is the perception of "duality" created with regard to our union with God. We need to better understand the idea of "divine inspiration" as one that supports free will and carries a greater sense of reality. We also need a greater comprehension of our union with the Creator. Many of the Christian mystics taught a non-dual concept of the Creator and creation. I believe their picture of "being one with God" is the closest form of the ultimate truth we will find here on Earth. Western Christianity has created a dual concept between humankind and deity, an illusion that God and His creation are separate entities. This duality comes in spite of the "oneness" with God as insisted on in the scriptures. It may seem paradoxical that in terms of our visible understanding of reality, all of the Creation appears to be separate from God, and yet we are told in Scripture everything is one with God. We know it will appear blasphemous if we claim, "We are God," but many of the mystics believed that the divine omnipresence suggested an inseparable essence between God and creation. The scientific breakthrough of quantum mechanics in the late nineteenth and early twentieth centuries lent much credence to this notion.

The consensus amongst many of those in the burgeoning Consciousness Movement finds cohesion around the concept of singularity, an inseparable union between the "individual" human soul, the collective consciousness of all beings, and the consciousness of the Creator. It is implied that the consciousness of God is a type of universal source field that pervades all of Creation, and that the individuality of each soul is an illusion for the purpose of interaction with the created world. This further suggests that the soul is a combination of two inseparable "selves": the higher and the lower. It is maintained that human beings can find their higher self through a process of meditation, prayer, and right-relationship with the Creator.

The beautiful truth about this revelation is that all of us carry infinity within our souls and, much more than possessing a mere connection to the Creator, we are indeed one in essence with God. The idea of the wave function in quantum mechanics, now proved in laboratories, lends a powerful analogy to the understanding of the source field in which the entire creation resides.

*

The Bigger Picture

Ray's mention of a small window to start a new church would provide the eventual circumstance through which I would be delivered from my fundamentalist idealism, and pave the way for a glimpse of the bigger picture.

29: Starting Another Church? Really?

Adeline did not take to the idea of starting another church. She is so much more down to earth than I am. I do believe, however, that she understood the visionary in me; that I would never be happy outside of the ministry. Her pragmatic interpretation of my emotional wellbeing stemmed from the past thirty years of my dedicated and committed attitude toward God and the Church. I confess, however, that this fanatical behavior of dedication often brought me into conflict with who and what came first in any situation. Wherever possible, the Lord's Work always came before anything else, sometimes even to the detriment of my own family, a failing I deeply regret. I owe my wife and children so much for their ability to see past my shortcomings and over-zealousness, which often made them play second fiddle to the ministry. I labored under the false assumption that God would look after my family if I placed His work as a first priority. Although as a matter of principle Christians will always put God first in their lives, the practice of ministry as a lifestyle should not be considered above that of family needs. The family should always come first.

The Bigger Picture

I believe Adeline's eventual agreement to the new venture came as a response to her unhappiness with our situation in Pastor Brian's church. The move, moreover, promised an escape from his authoritarian ministry style. I, on the other hand, admired Pastor Brian's strong leadership abilities, and the only reason why I considered it necessary for us to jump ship rested in the fact that it gave me back the opportunity to be in charge of my own destiny—my supposed "calling" into God's work. Adeline and I both worked at jobs which would not be affected by an involvement with a new ministry. For me, it came as an answer to the ponderous idea of insurance sales for the rest of my days. As Ray suggested at the time, my past ability in the establishment of New Beginnings Church in South Africa assumed future successes. A biblical phrase came to mind: "All things are possible with God."

My two sons, Paul and Andrew, well established in their respective careers with the cable company, earned above average wages and enjoyed a great work environment. My daughter Alison's advancement in the IT profession in Houston, Texas, showed huge promise for her future and it remained for Adeline and I to stabilize our financial position, to balance the family financial equation. I saw this new opportunity to be the answer to my "called-of-God" dilemma, and so we threw ourselves into the new work with herculean efforts.

Colin Setterfield

A new venue to hold our meetings became the first item on our establishment agenda, and this materialized through a friend of the Kendricks. This friend who owned a building in which he ran a business for some years before his divorce, gave us permission to use the venue for our church services, and Living Waters Church came into being.

Our first meeting hosted eleven worshippers, a gaggle of new members, plus a few interested parties. I led the worship with my guitar, as in past times at home group meetings and the initial establishment of the New Beginnings Church in South Africa. After the sermon, Sheila and Justin Kendrick gave no indication of opposition to my leadership role, and everyone enjoyed the meeting. Over the next few months, the fledgling church grew to twenty-five people, inclusive of four children in the Sunday school.

In May of that same year, my brother Robert and sister-in-law, Eleanor, flew out from South Africa to spend five weeks with us and to attend my son Andrew's wedding. The other twin, Paul, married earlier in November 1995. An interesting fact about the twins: both boys married girls named Carrie, and the girls' parents were both named Jim and Linda. I could tell many interesting stories about identical twins. In their younger days and identical in every way—mirrored twins, they played many a trick on their teachers and peers. Any freckle-type moles or skin marks that appeared on one side of Paul's body appeared on the opposite side of Andrew's body. They separated for the first time at the age of seventeen when Paul entered his military training and Andrew began his college tuition. Over the period of this separation, both boys began to experience emotional problems; Paul came down with an undiagnosed illness and spent a few days in a military hospital, where a chaplain visited him. The chaplain discovered that Paul suffered separation anxiety, a well-known malady suffered by identical twins. Adeline and I received a call from the chaplain to explain that he knew the reason for Paul's undiagnosed illness: he missed his brother.

I concurred with the suggestion, as it became evident to me that Andrew suffered from depression. Adeline, Andrew and I, accompanied by Alison and Mike, then took five days off and made the 500 kilometer journey to Paul's military base situated in the Orange Free State. We all spent time together, after which the two boys perked up with considerable enthusiasm. I can testify to the fact that since that time, neither have been separated from the other for more than a month or two and have always lived in close proximity to each other. When one could not fulfill a certain aspect of his work for any reason, the other twin would stand in, and no one ever knew the difference. To this day, their friends still struggle with who is who.

After the initial two years of our residence in Canada both boys refused continued church attendance. I understood their reasoning behind the change in attitude because their childhood, ensconced in the fundamentalist Christian environment from a very young age, revealed the often flakiness and shallowness of many believers. The name of my old friend, Derek, pastor of the Eternal Life Church in South Africa, popped up several times in the conversations I had with Paul and Andrew about their church attendance. Pastor Derek's name also came up as an example of "lording it over others", from my daughter Alison's point of view. This is often the case with minister's children who see and hear the worst of things in church work. Our particular journey as a family, over the time of my ministry, crossed the difficult terrain of human reaction based more on pride and prejudice than the practice of biblical values. Despite all my justifications in favor of the Lord's protection of his children, plus the confession of my own negligence in not doing due diligence in the purchase of the business, it came as a pill too hard for them to swallow. I felt I couldn't lay blame when I reviewed the many hours of teaching bestowed on the subject of God's protection of His people.

*

Our fledgling church continued to grow. After six months we asked permission of the building's owner, one of our newest members, if we could make a few alterations to the main room used for the services, and he agreed. We incorporated a small kitchen, built in two more toilets, and separated the front area, which used to be the business reception. In addition, we sectioned off a part of the main hall for a Sunday School room, and altered the original reception area to accommodate a small apartment for a single tenant.

A door, cut into the sidewall of the building, provided a new entrance and we laid wall to wall carpet in the main hall. Thirty new chairs provided extra seating for new members and visitors. I discovered that a large community of people, who no longer attended church due to all the splits and commotions, existed in the city

Toward the end of that first year, I received a surprise before the start of a Sunday morning service when a couple, whom I shall call Harvey and Caroline, walked in through the front entrance to take two seats near the back. I recognized them as leaders from Pastor Brian's church. Adeline and I knew this couple to be his most ardent supporters and it puzzled me as to why they would attend one of our meetings. By this time, Pastor Brian's church, a lively fellowship with a good number of young people, no longer fellowshipped in their home due to the acquisition of an old cinema for a venue, which paid handsome dividends in the form of increased membership. I realized the matter of this couple's defection would be a hard pill for Pastor Brian to swallow, as Harvey, a wealthy real estate developer, provided good financial support for the ministry.

Another problem this unusual visit brought to my door would be Pastor Brian's attitude toward me as a colleague in the Lord's Work. He and I met every Monday morning for prayer, and I valued his fellowship. I did not want him to think I carried some complicity in Harvey and Caroline's decision to leave his church. After the service, Adeline and I singled Harvey and Caroline out at the refreshment bar; and the four of us, with cups of coffee in hand, settled down in a huddle near the back to have a chat. I'm not sure if I got to the root of their dissension, but the main problem appeared to be a loss of confidence in Pastor Brian's ministry and style of leadership. Harvey told us he wanted to leave when I first started the Living Waters ministry, but did not feel it would have been appropriate for him and Caroline to do so at the time. Harvey confided that he always felt, from the time he met me, that I had a "good word" to bring, and came across as a straight-shooter and compassionate soul.

I asked him a tough question. "Is it your intention to leave Brian's church, and does he know you're here this morning?"

Harvey looked pained. "It is our intention to leave, but we didn't say anything to Brian. We thought we would visit your church today and get a feel for the fellowship."

"How did you find the meeting?" I asked.

The Bigger Picture

"Like a breath of fresh air. I believe we could be very happy here," he answered.

I needed to impress a vital principle on Harvey. "You'll have to visit Pastor Brian and tell him of your intentions. He needs to have an opportunity to put right anything he might have done to offend you and Caroline."

Harvey nodded. "I understand. Caroline and I will pay him a visit tomorrow evening, but I don't think anything will change. We want to attend your service tonight if we may."

I assured them they were most welcome, and that I would talk to Pastor Brian at our early prayer the next morning to discuss the matter with him. Harvey and Caroline wanted to make the move on positive terms, so they agreed. Deep inside, I felt excited that we had gained them as members; but I also felt a tinge of sadness for Pastor Brian, because I thought the news would hit him hard. As pastors of newly established churches, neither of us could afford to lose members and building the church's financial base ensured the church's continued existence.

I attended the early prayer with Pastor Brian the next morning and told him about Harvey and Caroline's visit of the day before; his answer surprised me.

30: Gaining Some Influential Members

When I broached the subject of Harvey and Caroline's visit to our church, Pastor Brian did not seem surprised. "I guessed they might have paid you a visit when they weren't in church yesterday. Did they tell you why they want to leave?" he asked.

I wanted to be as truthful as I could be. "I couldn't get to the bottom of it, but for some reason, they appear to have lost confidence in your leadership. I told them they should come and talk to you privately before making any hasty decisions."

Pastor Brian shared that Harvey had not agreed with a decision on a short-term future project for their congregation. Harvey felt the expense involved would be a waste of their resources. In financial terms, as one of the leaders, he would have been expected to provide backing; but in his experience, he said, the project would limit the church's future growth.

Pastor Brian's calm acceptance of Harvey and Caroline's decision to leave his church and join the Living Waters Fellowship showed me he understood the intricate nuances of church membership dynamics. The incident did not alter our relationship and we continued to meet every Monday for early prayer.

The Bigger Picture

In July 2002, our venue revealed its limitations with a significant increase in our congregation membership; so Ray, Harvey, and I started to look for an alternate venue. Whatever building we chose needed to include church zoning, sufficient parking and the provision of adequate toilet facilities. Subsequent to a search that lasted about two weeks Harvey found a premises that appeared to hold some promise—a 10,000-square-foot venue in one of the city's strip malls. The space originally accommodated a large hardware store and the mall management, unable to fill the vacated area with a sizable business, entertained the dismal prospect of property tax payments on unproductive square footage. Harvey, an astute business person, saw the opportunity and asked if we could use the venue as a church. It seemed a little ambitious of us at the time, but the mall management agreed, and made a reasonable offer of first-year rent to be paid. At least their cost of city taxes would be covered, but our rent would increase by $1,000 a month after the first year.

I felt jittery about signing the contract, but Harvey said he would cover any shortfalls if anything went wrong; and besides, with the Lord's help, our church would grow enough to sustain the increased rent when it became payable. Ray also agreed so I stepped out in faith and signed the contract with the mall management. We still awaited confirmation on an agreement by the City to allow the premises to be used as a church. I attended several city council meetings, and after three months the city agreed to our use of the venue, provided we changed the designation of our business to "Ministries" and dropped the title of "Church." This came as my suggestion to the chairman in order to overcome the zoning issue which did not allow for church fellowships. The City agreed that an application for a church zoning would need to be made if we retained the venue over an extended period of time.

I now possessed a huge area in which to plan out our church operation. The main hall and entrance foyer, about 7,000 square feet, also provided several toilets and a mezzanine floor, which accounted for another 3,000 square feet. I found myself in project heaven! One year prior to our move into the new venue a change of job status came about for me when I resigned from North West Life in lieu of a contract with a non-profit organization that helped people on unemployment insurance find new work. I also started to receive a small stipend from the church to assist with the use of my vehicle in the ministry.

The evolving situation contained no frills, but both Adeline and I believed God would come through for us. My contract with the non-profit ended in December 2001, after which time I qualified for unemployment insurance. The church tithes picked up and in September 2002, when my employment insurance ran out, I drew small sums of money from the church to supplement our personal finances. Throughout the year 2003, I built the inside walls and decor of what became a beautiful venue for our main services. We placed a desk in the foyer, and one of the church ladies took on the position as church secretary, a five-day per week morning job, for which she donated her time. I had my own office and the eldership agreed on the purchase of two computers: one for me and one for the secretary. It felt much like New Beginnings Church in South Africa all over again. For me, it became tough going, as I spent much of the time, up to ten hours per day during the week, doing building work and painting walls. Apart from the two Sunday meetings, I took a bible study on Wednesday evenings and convened a fellowship prayer group on Thursdays nights. Help from Jason Kendrick and his eldest son, who carted building materials and did all the electrical work, constituted an invaluable service to the establishment of our venue.

My personal credit card became the means of our purchases, mostly building materials for which the church paid me back on a monthly basis. My biggest tithers in the work, Ray, Harvey, and Jason Kendrick, all pitched in with whatever help they could give me. During this time, I officiated at weddings and funerals, baptisms and church problems which needed my counsel; a hectic time until the completion of the building project.

My strong desire to establish a work through the performance of a ministry that catered to the spiritual needs of those who follow Christ lay rooted in my basic personality type (Meyers Briggs: INFJ)[29] and the need to be of service to others. My ministerial style reflected the many lessons learned from those whom I had become associated with over the decades of church involvement, lessons both good and bad. There are times when you get it right and times when you get it wrong. No one can claim perfection in leadership; this is true of all leaders, be it in the church, in politics, sport, business or any other type of activity. Leaders are human beings affected by their emotions and egos, just like everyone else. When I analyzed the positives of my main ministerial traits they would line up on the positive side as visionary, intuitive and empathetic, disciplined, and Word-directed. On the negative side: At times melancholic and prone to depression, a struggle with rejection, and certain egotistical issues. Not everyone agreed with my management style.

From time to time, people use a leader's efforts to further their own agendas or ambitions. This appeared to be the case with a couple whom I appointed as leaders of our singles group. The unmarried, divorced, and widowed folk in the church sought a time of their own for fellowship. When approached to establish a special meeting for these people, I worried that it might turn out to be a dating club, but I also saw a need for supporters of such a meeting to discuss, under supervision, the things that were pertinent to their single status. I relented—against my better judgment—and felt that the couple I placed in charge to be capable and trustworthy enough to handle the project.

The Bigger Picture

Three weeks after the meeting's establishment in the couple's home, I suffered a bad feeling about it, so I decided to drop in and check things out. Adeline and I arrived about ten minutes after the start of the meeting, and I immediately became aware that all the participants eyed us with a measure of hostility. No one greeted us, and some would not catch my eye as we tried to get a feel for the spirit of the meeting. The appointed leader stood up and announced a short time of prayer to precede the planned topic for the evening. He did not ask me if we wanted to be prayed for, but asked us to move our chairs to the center of the room so that the group could surround us. Adeline and I thought nothing to be amiss about the request until the group gathered around and laid hands on our shoulders. They started to pray, that I as the appointed pastor of the church, would receive the Lord's guidance in my management of the church and spiritual matters.

The prayers began to take on a personal tone. It would seem they thought me to be misguided in some of the doctrines I preached. This came as a surprise as no one in the church, up to that time, ever disagreed with what I believed. A very misguided, divorced woman prayed that the Lord would deliver me from my "South African ways," that Canadian ministers did things differently. Confused, I stood and asked the leader if I could talk to him outside. We stepped onto the driveway in the warm summer evening air, and another married couple joined us. They told me in no uncertain terms of their decision to break away from our church and start their own meetings with the single people. I felt betrayed. It would appear that from the start the initiative to do something for the singles came from the second married couple, who suggested to several of the divorcees that they ask for a separate meeting. Later it came to my ears that this couple, newer members of our church, caused trouble in all their previous places of worship.

We left the premises and headed home in a state of shock. I chided myself on a lack of attentiveness to my gut feeling when first asked to allow such a meeting to be convened. We lost twenty-two members through that incident. The rest of the church could not believe their ears when I made a formal statement about the event. I later called both couples in question, hoping to speak to them further about the deceitful action, but neither would speak with me. Talk about wolves amongst the sheepfold! I approached the congregation to be honest with me with any ways that appeared to be "South African" and they all with one accord, affirmed my ministry. No one understood the accusation and we all decided to put the matter behind us.

Another incident over a couple, not married in the traditional way and who cohabited together, caused a stir amongst the more legal-minded members of the church, came into fellowship with us. I understood that a few of the members might not approve of this couple, but in our modern age most open-minded

The Bigger Picture

Christians accepted that we lived in times of change. Two couples, however, took umbrage at my position, one of them being the Kendricks; they cited the fundamental biblical position that this couple would bring disrepute to our church. Mrs. Kendrick, the one who wanted her pastor friend to return and take our church over, became very vocal about the matter. I knew she entertained some very legalistic ideas from her Pentecostal roots, but apart from a few rumblings about the charismatic nature of our worship style, the family kept its peace. A week later, sadly, the Kendrick family left the church for greener pastures.

Once people feel they have been disillusioned in some way, an attempt to convince them otherwise or change their minds does not help. It is one of those times when you, as a pastor, second guess yourself, but the rest of the church appeared to be okay with the status quo, so I let it go. To banish this "unmarried" couple from the church as requested by the Kendricks (and a few others) would have been, in my eyes, a travesty of real justice and a betrayal of real values. While the couple in question did not possess a formal contract of marriage their legal status in the eyes of the law lay within the parameters of "common law". I maintained that true marriage remains a matter of the heart, a promise between the couple and the Lord. In former times the family decided on the validity of a marriage, not the government of the day. I understand, however, the difficulty for some people to grasp the spirit of it.

Colin Setterfield

*

I thought the adversity we faced in the wake of the church's establishment would end, but a rocky road still lay ahead of us.

31: The Ebb and Flow of Membership

The arrival of a new couple, owners of a small business in the mall, offset the loss of the Kendricks. This new couple, whom I shall call Rob and Crystal, would watch the congregation members stream into the church for Sunday meetings, intrigued by the jovial talk and laughter of people who appeared to enjoy their time together. One Sunday, prior to the morning service Ray spotted the couple at the door of their business and engaged them in conversation. Rob commented on our group of ardent motorcyclists who met on most Saturday and Sunday afternoons in front of the church building for a recreational ride. The fact that a group of "bible-punchers" rode bikes fascinated them. The new couple also owned a motorcycle, and expressed an interest to ride with us so Ray invited them to meet with our group after the morning service. Rob and Crystal expressed, at a later date, that they became fascinated by our joyful banter and apparent cohesiveness to the point where they saw us as "normal folk" and not as a group of "holier than thou" church goers. On the Sunday that followed our group ride Ray invited Rob and Crystal to attend the morning service.

Around this time Harvey suffered some significant financial losses in his real estate development business. The real estate development committee of an adjacent community, where Harvey wanted to build two hundred new homes, never let on that they frowned upon such a large development; Instead they strung Harvey along for three years, a period in which he invested a lot of money for infrastructure, but the council always threw in an obstacle before a building permit could be granted. In the end, in a state of utter frustration, Harvey decided to abandon the project and sell up the assets. This decision amounted to a huge loss of investment in purchase of architectural plans, building application fees and pre-building preparations. To recoup some of the investment amounted to one of two directions: the sale of the land with the inclusion of all costs in the form of a viable project, or sell the land and abandon the incurred costs. I never discovered which of these two directions he took, but he and Caroline decided to leave us and head for the mainland in the hope of involvement with a more sympathetic municipality, perhaps a form of financial salvation for them but a huge loss for our church.

The safety net with regard to our rental agreement evaporated into thin air and Harvey's original promise of financial back-up in the event of unforeseen circumstances seemed hollow and distant. The church, about to lose two of its most influential members, also faced the loss of a significant tithe, one which underpinned a part of the church's budget. I realized that unless we found more members, the second year's expected rent obligation could not be met. From experience I also knew that my own personal stipend would need to be reduced to accommodate a drop in the church's income. This is a reality all pastor's involved in church establishment must face and be prepared for. Adeline worked for a financial planner as an office manager, but her income could not carry all of our personal needs. I needed a new financial plan.

Rob and Crystal, our newest members, showed a heightened interest in the Christian faith so I invited them to my home one Saturday morning to explain our basic beliefs. I explained the "way of salvation" to them and they both accept the Lord into their hearts. The inclusion of new people never failed to create an excitement amongst the rest of the congregation, and everyone perceived it to be a favorable sign from God.

Rob, Crystal, and I became great friends. With their business right next door to the church, we gained easy access to one another, and I poured as much of my spirit into them as I could. Rob picked up on an old talent acquired as a young man—the electric guitar; and within a short space of time, he joined our church's music group. Crystal possessed a marginal singing voice, so Ray, permitted her to sing along with the band. Rob and Crystal took to the church scene like ducks to water, and became ardent supporters of the faith.

By the end of that year the financial situation, strained to the limit, gave me cause for alarm; although we showed a small growth in membership, the general tithes lacked Harvey's generous contributions. I took less and less financial support in order to keep the church viable. The beginning of the new rental year brought the anticipated increase of $1,000 per month, and the budget wilted under the increased load. I approached the mall management to see what we could arrange. The one brother (of the landlord duo) with whom I enjoyed a good rapport assured me things would pan out; he told me not to worry about the increase.

"Just pay what you have been paying. My brother and I will speak to our father and see if we can't come to some arrangement," he said.

This matter never came up again in our occasional conversations, and I thought that the owners might give us a break on the rent. My mistake. The situation would come back to bite me at the end of that rental year. The ministry continued on, and the church leadership never gave the matter another thought. I performed several weddings amongst couples who came to me for counsel, but not all of these young people became members. People are what they are, and once they have achieved their agenda, they often lost interest in spiritual matters. I helped many people who could not afford a removal service to move homes. On at least two occasions, we supplied the funds for cube van rentals, after which the families in question never returned and despite my attempts to contact them they disappeared into the great blue yonder.

This type of behavior I found to be fairly common amongst the needy segment of the population. Such people often developed a welfare mentality, where they expected all their needs to be taken care of by the community. I recall a particular case of a single mother with two children who came to a Sunday morning service with her kids in tow. One of the congregants who spoke to her at length discovered that she faced eviction from her semi-detached apartment. After receipt of the notice the woman found an apartment in the city into which she could move her family but lacked the finances to cover the cost of the move. The member approached me to see if we could help in any way and I responded positively to say we would help her move out of the present home and into a new apartment. Ray's father-in-law offered to help me out with the move, which took place a few days later. I rented a cube van and we arrived at her address, ready to move all the furniture and personal effects.

When we walked into the apartment, I realized the cause for her eviction. The place, in a total mess, revealed that this young woman exercised little control over the sloven habits of her family. Dirty plates filled the kitchen sink and the stove top splattered with various ingredients, required a good clean. It appeared no one took any thought to wipe down the countertops or kitchen cabinets and dirty clothes lay every where on the floors; the dust almost suffocated me. But a greater shock awaited us. The woman told me that her fourteen-year-old son suffered from autism, and never allowed anyone into his room. While we stood and waited she took her son aside and explained to him that we would require access to the room in order to move out all his belongings. He put up a fight but after some bargaining by his mother he relented.

Ray's father-in-law and I stepped into the room with unfeigned gasps of horror. Half-filled plates of food covered every available flat surface, which included the floor. Clothes lay strewn everywhere and the bedding stank of urine. I should have walked out at that moment and told her to find someone else, but this would not have been good Christian conduct. We moved their belongings and discovered even more filth than anticipated. Scuff marks on the walls, food stains on the carpets, and dusty light fittings, painted a scene of total neglect. At the end of our day from hell I beat a retreat to my home for a much-needed shower, and made every attempt to disinfect my body.

Of course, the woman advocated the need to turn over a new leaf and promised future dedication to church attendance, plus counsel, to get her life back on track. The assurances rolled off her tongue with too much ease and I detected a spirit of deception. She did not even thank us for our effort on the day of the move, an omission that revealed her spirit of entitlement. After

The Bigger Picture

two weeks of her non-attendance, punctuated by numerous attempts to make contact, I felt constrained to report the case to Social Welfare. Those two children could not continue on in such conditions. She never did come back to church.

Rob and Crystal employed a friend in their business, whom I shall call Dawn, and who lived on the outskirts of the city on a three-acre lot. Dawn, a divorcee, stayed on her own in a leak-prone, derelict modular home, way past its prime. She possessed a limited amount of money for a new house to be built on the property, but not enough to employ a contractor to do the job. Rob, out of work but with a good deal of construction experience under his belt offered to build the small home for a reduced price, so I offered to help as much as I could with the project. It took us about three months of extremely hard work to get the new building to a move-in status for Dawn. In all that time, I worked side by side with Rob, and never asked for any form of personal compensation because I knew he and Crystal did not have much money. It suffices to say that Dawn became a member of the church after that.

Rob and Crystal, both in possession of giving natures, would invite me each weekday for lunch and we enjoyed many good times of fellowship together. In compensation I made sure that my new friends learned everything I could teach them about the faith.

At the end of the contractual year, the mall management paid me a visit one morning and dropped a bombshell.

"We have found a tenant who is prepared to pay the full amount of rent per square foot for your space. You will have to come up with the full amount if you want to continue. If not, your lease ends at the end of this month. If you need it, we will give you one extra month to find a new venue."

I was devistated. I entertained an ambitious vision to purchase the entire strip mall one day when our growth into a mega-sized operation became a reality, but in retrospect this aspiration stemmed from my earlier days of involvement with the prosperity movement.

I glared at the two brothers. "We can't even afford to pay the annual increase—how do you expect us to come up with ten times that amount?" I answered.

The one brother raised his eyebrows. "I understand your predicament, but you must realize we are businessmen, and we can't afford to subsidize you when there is someone who will pay the full amount. You also still owe us the increase in rent for the past twelve months, and we cannot afford to forgive that amount."

Stunned by the landlord's comments I contemplated the loss of our venue, plus the investment of a considerable amount of money to turn it into a church facility. On top of all that we still

The Bigger Picture

owed the mall $12,000! I told the two gentlemen that we could not pay the new rent and would make plans to move out at the end of that month. I also needed time to speak to the leadership to see what we could do about the back rent. My thoughts wandered back to the fast-food business, our first venture in Canada, and a horrible truth presented itself: I appeared to have no luck with businesses in malls. The question uppermost in my mind: where did God feature in all this?

I arranged a meeting with the rest of our leadership and explained the problem. Ray suggested we approach the movie theaters in town to find a possible venue. No one came up with an immediate answer for the back rent, so I decided to take the contract to a lawyer, to see if a way out of our dilemma might present itself; no such luck. We needed a new venue so I called the Galaxy group of theaters, situated in one of the big malls in the city, and received a favorable response from the manager. If our income remained steady, we might even be able to service the back rent debt, and I could still continue to draw a small amount for personal support.

I didn't realize at the time that even greater difficulties awaited Living Waters Church—circumstances that would threaten its very existence.

32: An Awkward Confrontation

In 2003 my daughter Alison, resident in Houston, Texas, USA, visited us. Her husband Mike couldn't make it due to work constraints, but she brought our grandchild, Kaitlin, then five years old, with her. While in discussion of mutual interests Alison shared some very interesting facts about scientific discoveries in the realm of quantum physics.[30] I had no idea at that stage what the word "quantum" meant, but what she said intrigued me enough to buy a book on the subject. I read about the history of the scientists and founders of the weird phenomenon with regard to experiments in particle physics. As a young man in my early twenties, I developed a fondness for the genre of science fiction and at the time the concept of space travel and the physical sciences captivated my imagination. My involvement in fundamental religion, however, put a quick damper on that interest.

To emphasize the bondage our first church experience placed us under, the elders and pastors preached against science and made it out to be a construct of the devil. According to our church, anyone who read the genre did so at their peril, and the eventual loss of the soul. Prior to our first church experience Adeline and I watched the movie 2001: A Space Odyssey in late

The Bigger Picture

1968, a movie I enjoyed at the time and will never forget. Two years later, when I gave my life to Jesus, one of the aspects of that film—a portrayal of the theory of evolution, which represented another supposed devil's doctrine—reinforced the notion of science fiction as an unholy pursuit.

The executives of our denomination frowned upon any interests that lay beyond acceptable religious beliefs. Any believer involved in such practices risked the wrath of the eldership. I stopped all attendance of movie theaters, and never read another secular book, for at least ten years. It should be included here that I read every Christian book on history and theology I could get my hands on, and continued that practice for the next thirty years.

My foray into quantum physics opened up a fascination for the fabric of spacetime, a new world of science for me. While I'm not an expert on the phenomenon, I have read widely, and my Kindle electronic reader is loaded with more than a dozen books on the subject. One salient fact I gleaned from the quantum world is that every particle in the universe retains an awareness and knows when it is being observed. All sorts of scientific theories flowed from the behavior of particles, in an "entangled" state or "superposition,"[31] the proof of which again reignited my penchant for the physical sciences. The weird behavior of particles allows them to be in more than one place at any time, and when not observed by the human mind, particles exist in the form of a wave. When observed (through sensitive equipment) the wave function collapses into a particle to represent the material structure we see with the naked eye. New theories of parallel universes, multiverses, and the existence of different cosmic dimensions flowed from the strange particle behavior in the quantum world. It did much to whet my appetite and better understand the mysteries that surround our universe.

Then came the Hubble Space Telescope,[32] which opened up the avenues of astrophysics,[33] astrobiology,[34] and cosmology.[35] The word "cosmos" is not well received amongst Fundamental Christians, because of its occultist connotation. Translated from the Greek word "Kosmos," cosmology is the study of the origin and evolution of our universe, which before Hubble left astronomers at the mercy of Earth-based telescopes, hampered by the problem of atmospheric distortions. The advent of Hubble stoked the fires of astrophysics, astrobiology, and exobiology, sciences that reveal the life and death cycle of stars and the evolution of life in the universe. My mind exploded with the array of possibilities of how different our real evolutionary path might be from the biblical explanations I held as ultimate truth. I began to look for explanations of life in greater terms of reality, and for the first time in my career as a minister, the abundance of historical record that lay outside of religious influences, became an interest that begged greater research.

The Bigger Picture

I struggled to keep most of this out of my preaching, because I knew the legalists, would take umbrage at the mix of religion and science if I dared to preach on such topics. The sudden realization that all my knowledge of Christianity stemmed from Christian authors and teachers who denounced what mainstream science taught, hit me like a hammer. Much of what I learned through my years of Bible study stopped short of any proof as ratified by actual history and the real world. This epiphany resulted in a study of the role played by religion through the ages, and it soon became apparent that religions often directly, or indirectly, caused many tragic and atrocious events throughout the history of humankind. Much of the unrest that exists in certain parts of the world today are as a direct result of religious tensions. I started to see organized religion in a different light, a dangerous occupation for an ordained minister in a fundamental setting.

*

Living Waters Church moved out of the strip mall and into the movie theatre in June, 2004. All the decor of our past venture awaited removal by the new tenant, a provider of children recreational services. I arranged for the sale of the chairs, office desks and tables, and plowed the proceeds into our building fund, which elevated the fund to about $3,000. The mall management said nothing further about the debt, and I was happy to leave it be in the hope that some miracle would save us from the $12,000 owed on the back rent.

Two months later, Ray, Janet, Rob, Crystal, Adeline and I decided to take a ten-day motorcycle trip, and we left for the mainland. The other church leaders took over and ran the Sunday morning meetings on my behalf. We divided the congregation up into two home group meetings, which took place on Wednesday nights. The music group placed all their equipment into a large wooden box which Rob and I made for the purpose and we found a place for the box in the back corridor which serviced the rear of the theaters. Ray canceled the usual Thursday night music practice in favor of an hour prior to the Sunday meeting, which worked well enough for the musicians.

Come September, I pondered a new idea. The local Seventh Day Adventist Church possessed their own building in the city, and required a tenant to rent the building on Sundays, to supplement the mortgage. Another mainline church, about the same size as our fellowship, occupied the basement hall, serviced by a separate entrance. Together, with the other tenant, we accessed the single kitchen downstairs, adjacent to the basement hall, an arrangement both groups came to appreciate and enjoy. Our respective service times coincided well enough for a short post-service communal fellowship over refreshments. The arrangement suited us, and we moved from the theater to the Adventist church building. Our presence did not affect the Adventists because their prime service took place on Saturday mornings. They also allowed us to use the church on any other evening other than a Saturday. We started up music practices on Thursday evenings again, an arrangement welcomed by the musicians.

December brought the Sumatra Tsunami tragedy, which took the lives of more than 200,000 people in that region. Our church galvanized to send money for the relief fund, which countries all over the world supported. The new year and new premises promised growth for the future, and I decided to set a more evangelistic tone to the ambiance of our meetings. The introduction of a Bible Study on urban evangelism raised the ire of some of the members who didn't feel the need for active evangelism. My vision, however, rested on a steady growth in numbers which extrapolated into the type of finance required for a long-term, sustainable outreach to the community. We required people who desired a deeper spiritual experience, and who could support the eventual purchase of land and erection of a large worship center. This is what my estranged South African colleague, Pastor Derek, taught as the recipe for success, a principle also followed by the pastors of the many mega-churches throughout the world. I believed growth to be the key to success. I now realize this is not true for all situations, but at the time it appeared to be the only dynamic that would save our church from mediocrity and eventual decline.

With our move of venues came a subtle change in my relationship with Rob and Crystal. We no longer shared that close proximity of their business to the church. I noticed the development of a closer friendship between Ray and Rob, and the two couples often visited with each other. In my long-term relationship with Ray he never, in all the years, cultivated a friendship with such complete abandonment of boundaries. I became concerned that he and Rob might foster an unhealthy situation which could blow up in their faces and affect the church in a negative way. I noticed the two couples would arrive late for meetings, and then often leave before the meeting concluded. At first, not always being available, I thought the mutual relationship might be beneficial for Rob and Crystal's spiritual growth and that Ray's experience offered a supplementary perspective.

The two couples continued to visit each other, and I can't recall that I ever saw them apart. One Sunday service, on the arrival at the church, both men sported peroxided hair. It surprised me no end as Ray's prior conservative attitude, in the norm, excluded such vain actions. He possessed a genius for organization, worked hard at any project allotted to him, and always earned very good money in his sphere of employment. Ray's A-type personality meant he brooded a lot, maintained an angry attitude about life in general, and often displayed a skeptical view toward life. I always joked with Adeline, that Ray lived his life at DEFCON 1. He did, however, have a contagious sense of humor, and provided an invaluable source of encouragement to those who suffered hardships. I remember when Adeline and I lost our business, Ray took the time to call me every day to dispense positive encouragement, and I appreciated him for it.

I received a flurry of negative comments from the congregation with regard to the peroxided hair incident. One member asked me if Ray and Rob might have converted to an alternative lifestyle, and another called them the "pretty twins." This polarization became difficult for me to handle, and after a few more weeks of the couples late arrivals and early departures, I made an appointment to visit Ray and Janet at their home. Neither Adeline nor I could fathom what had come over Ray and Rob, but it needed to be brought to a head.

We arrived after dinner time at Ray and Janet's home on the evening of the planned visit. I knew their guard would be up, because of my request that Rob and Crystal not be present. I wanted to talk to them alone. If the need arose, I would talk to Rob and Crystal on a separate occasion. After a few moments of small talk, I shared the real reason for my visit. Ray became very irate with me and accused me of meddling in his private affairs. He insisted the two couples got on well with each other, and that their friendship existed within acceptable boundaries. I pointed out that he (Ray) held an important position as lead elder in the work, a position of authority that carried a major responsibility in the eyes of the congregation. Their continuous late arrivals and early departures created the impression of disregard for normal church protocols. In conjunction, while peroxided hair did not constitute a crime, it should be understood that such actions might solicit negative comments from others. Both Ray and Janet refused to see the point and continued to justify their position. They accused me of a change of attitude toward the ministry in general; that my disciplinary approach with the congregation did not in any way endear me to the members.

I performed a quick mental inventory of my dealings with some of the more flaky members, and concluded there might be a measure of truth in Ray's observation. In any long-term ministry, certain inconsistencies and lax attitudes portrayed by some of the congregants can create a sense of disillusionment for many pastors. I believed that a weariness due from all the loss experienced since my arrival in Canada, clutched at my soul. I thanked Ray for his observation and we all calmed down.

I hoped we both learned something of value from the confrontation. The entire event weighed on my conscience with such a heaviness that I decided to take a week off to visit our church flow's area supervisor. All the churches in our group claimed autonomy, but to prevent leaders from going their own course, pastors sought the oversight of a man whose ministry everyone considered to be apostolic. Such a man, Pastor Glen,

The Bigger Picture

and I, became good friends over the course of Living Waters' tenure. Pastor Glen resided in Saskatchewan and ran a thriving church of his own. Adeline could not come with me due to work constraints, so I jumped on my motorcycle and made the trip alone. It turned out to be a worthwhile time of fellowship, and I returned a week later, refreshed and ready to take up the baton again. A few dark weeks, however, still lay ahead.

Colin Setterfield

33: Music Group Mutiny

A few weeks later on a Saturday evening, Adeline and I visited Ray and Janet for a barbecue. I hoped it to have been limited to the four of us; but on arrival, we found Rob and Crystal also present. Ray's home overlooked the Georgia Straits, and we sat outside on the verandah around a table, in enjoyment of the beautiful view.

Ray, who sat next to me, made a request. "Do you think you can find someone to take my place as overseer of the music?"

His question took me by surprise. "Why? You've always enjoyed doing it, and have done such a good job."

"I just need to spend more time at home," he said.

"Okay, I'll see what I can do. I can't think of anyone else I'd like to see in that position, but I'll get onto it."

I didn't want to lose Ray's organizational and leadership abilities, but if he wanted out from the music oversight, then it would not be fruitful for either of us if I insisted he stay on. Our time-tested relationship, based on mutual interest and respect, now appeared to be under stress. It concerned me that too much familiarity over the years might have bred a measure of contempt between us. After some prayer and contemplation I couldn't think of anyone else who would perform the job of the music oversight as well as Ray, so I decided to step into the position and allow him the freedom he sought.

I called a meeting of the musicians after the next Sunday service to tell them of Ray's request to be released from the music group, and that I would be take his place. The look of dismay on the faces of the musicians, told its own story. The following Thursday night at music practice, Rob asked if he could speak to me in private, so we adjourned to the baby's cry room for the privacy he sought.

Rob folded his arms in a confrontational stance. "Why have you dropped Ray from the oversight role?"

"Because he asked me to release him," I replied.

"Not according to him," answered Rob. "Why are you deliberately scattering the sheep?"

I looked at him in surprise. "Why on Earth would you say something like that?"

His next words stunned me. "I've heard all about your dealings with the singles who all left because they didn't think the church was properly run. Then there's that case about the couple living in sin; you wrote that booklet on marriage to justify their continued fellowship with us—only a few people actually agree with your theology. You want us to support your efforts to grow the church, but you are chasing people away. Now you've dropped Ray from the music. What's next? His position as an elder?"

I assured Rob that I would never start a church with the intention of sabotaging it. The people who left did so because they had another agenda. Rob, still a novice in Christian terms, now wanted to expose demons that didn't exist. It would appear that I, a veteran of over three decades of church involvement, did not know how to run a fellowship! There is enough humility in me to not pull rank on anyone who questions my authority, but Rob's accusations got under my skin. A deep sadness flooded my soul as I thought of the many hours spent on Rob and Crystal's spiritual growth, plus the opportunities provided to be involved in the music ministry, not to mention Dawn's building project. Now I'm told by this greenhorn that I don't know how to run a ministry, plus I have chased people away!

I loved Rob and did not want to belittle his paltry knowledge of spiritual matters, so I said one thing to end the confrontation. "If you think I'm really that bad, then you had better pray for me. After all, I am your pastor, and only a human being. I know my faults and to be clear, none of them are as destructive in the manner you are suggesting."

Rob's retort to my reason for Ray's release from the music confused me. Why would Ray tell him a lie? It didn't make sense. I needed to speak to Ray before the matter developed any

The Bigger Picture

further. That opportunity never presented itself. Janet came to me at the end of that evening's music practice to say they would be going to Hawaii for a week and that her parents, both in the music group, plus Rob and Crystal, would go with them.

"You'll have to run the music for the next two Sunday meetings, as the worship leader will also be away," said Janet.

I should have held my tongue, but the rules with regard to involvement in the music ministry, came to the fore. "We all decided, as our personal commitment to the ministry, to always have a minimum of at least six people available every Sunday. If you all go off to Hawaii, that leaves only two others, and it will affect the presentation of worship for the rest of the congregation."

"I know we said that," said Janet. "But we have already booked the flights, and the arrangement can't be changed now."

I felt so let down. I appeared to be the only one interested in the future of Living Waters Church. Again, I should have held my tongue, but I didn't. I guess I'm human after all. "I will have to think about your future involvement with the music if that's the course you guys are on."

"That's fine with us. We can talk about it when we get back," she said.

A deep hole awaited my next step. Although I entertained reservations about the music to be offered for the weekend in question, I would never have dropped anyone from the group. Adeline and I, together with the remaining music group member, would have to carry the torch until the others returned from their vacation. We detected a conspiratorial atmosphere amongst those who joined Ray and Janet on the Hawaii trip. Perhaps they wanted to show me I could not do without them. It never occurred to me, at the time, they would leave the church but I stood to be corrected.

On their return from the Hawaiian trip, Ray sent me an email of resignation from the church. I replied with a suggestion that we get together to talk about it, but he declined. It appeared to be the end of a long and fruitful association. The reasons he gave confused me, and I couldn't make sense of their sudden change in attitude. Rob called me at home and also tendered his resignation. I sat speechless at my desk. The ministry appeared to be disintegrating. Despite my attempts, no one wanted to listen to reason, so I locked myself in my office at home and shed tears of frustration.

At the next Sunday meeting, Janet's parents approached me and handed in their set of church keys. They told me in no uncertain terms that they wouldn't be back, and I could run the church any way I wanted—but it would be on my own. That evening, I received a call from the music leader, the person whose building we initially used to start the work in, who tendered his resignation as well. I counted a total of eight key peo-

The Bigger Picture

ple who no longer wanted to be a part of Living Waters Church. The economic implications didn't sink in at the time, but when given some thought, the stark realization hit me on the head. Due to the departure of the music group a huge drop in income now jeopardized the payment of the church bills. I needed a plan to ensure the church's survival. It also became clear to me that the abdications by the music group must have been planned over a period of time. Not only did this apparent deceitfulness hurt, but I placed the blame upon myself. The fault did not lie with the music group, but with me; after all, it is the founder-leader who must take the responsibility. My long-term ministerial effort lay in tatters.

None of the remaining members shared my self-deprecation, but blamed Ray and Janet for the break-away. The remnant of the Living Waters membership rallied around to affirm my ministry and enveloped me in a cloak of love. Many testified to my years of competent counsel and the encouragement engendered through Sunday sermons. Despite this accolade of support, I broke out with shingles as a result of all the stress and strain. Even the loss of the business in 1996 paled in the face of this disaster. My call of God and future ministry faced a test never before envisaged, but hope of resurrection still lingered.

The final blow, however, landed a day later. I received a letter from the mall landlords who threatened legal action over our back-rent debt. They demanded that the $12,000 be paid within twenty-one days. The brothers instructed me to make contact before they took legal action to recover the deficit. As things stood, I did not have enough income to pay the current rent, or myself, so I decided to do the next best thing: I laid myself off as pastor of the church and applied for unemployment insurance. For the sake of the official record, I made Adeline the principle elder in the work. With her salary, we could afford to eat, but for the second time since our arrival in Canada, a reduction in monthly living expenses became necessary to make ends meet.

I called the Adventist pastor and explained the position. We came to an agreement in terms of a reduced rent. It amazed him that so many people could leave without any thought of the financial repercussions to the church. The mall managers met with me a few days later to discuss the back rent.

While sympathetic to my position they insisted on the payment of the money within the mandated period. Our building fund stood at about $3000, a quarter of the amount of the debt, so I decided to make an offer—which, to my surprise, they accepted. It required that I pay over the amount in the building fund, plus a few thousand dollars to be raised by the congregation. The remainder of the membership, not affluent enough to be of help, came up with about $800.00, so yours truly drew out the remainder on his credit card.

I did my best to allay bitter thoughts towards those who stood by me at the time of signing the rental agreement. Because

The Bigger Picture

my signature appeared on the contract, I alone held the cookie jar. A default on the debt payment, however, would have the mall managers pursue every name listed on the directorship, perhaps the provision of a just ending to the saga; but the thought of God's name being dragged through the courts of law did not seem right to me. Life goes on.

Colin Setterfield

34: Picking up the Pieces

The walkout by the music group provided me with the final straw that broke the back of my ardent belief in the inherent goodness of human nature. I know this sounds like an immature reaction for someone so long on the Christian road, but the losses up to that point shook my confidence in the God of the Bible. It made me think deeply about my beliefs—a subtle turn of the tide. My path through life appeared to have reached the limit of its flow, and only the ebb remained. Although the rest of the congregation gave their whole hearted support the loss of Christian joy due to the actions of the music group walkout hung like a dark cloud over the meetings. Our remnant viewed the musicians with a measure of contempt, and it seemed incomprehensible to them that good Christians would do such things to one another, but as I explained to them, the outcome reflected the potential of any group dynamic.

Determined not to give up, I made a valiant effort to mend fences and pull things together, but the fellowship would never be the same again. With the departure of the competent musicians, I, took over the leadership of the music and began to lead the meetings in worship. In the week that followed the walkout,

The Bigger Picture

I appointed two more people to the music ministry to do vocals. Our drummer, not a part of the walkout, placed his drums aside and picked up a guitar for extra accompaniment and in the beginning, the shingles, which attacked one shoulder and my neck area, made it very difficult for me to lead with my guitar. After a week, the medication began to kick in enough to deal with the pain, and a month later the condition passed. We grew in our new ministries and handled the music in a professional way.

Double work for me. We now arrived much earlier to set up the equipment and have a short practice before the service started. At the end of each worship session, I would have someone do the announcements before the sermon. The fellowship remained at around twenty-three people, about a quarter of its size during the good years. The original leadership team set out, in the beginning, to establish a great work for God, but it appeared the prime deity no longer held any interest in the work. I became more cognizant of church group dynamics and what it took to hold things together through the duration of the many religious storms that beset such gatherings. We always believed that the Holy Spirit and the bonds of God's love, held our relationships together but in the end, it all came down to how we treated each other in situations of disagreement. I believe my good friends, Ray and Janet, made a decision to end our seventeen-year relationship, based on the notion that I, in some way, disillusioned them. I called Ray and Rob out on their behavior in an attempt to save them the inevitable rush to judgement by their church colleagues, but I guess it backfired on me. Perhaps Ray thought it unfair of me to point out the obvious and construed it as an attack on his character, but this was not something I would ever have done to a trusted friend; my real intensions lay in the protection of the fellowship as a whole. Over the thirteen years that have since passed, up to the writing of this manuscript, neither of us has reached out to the other. It is as though neither of us exists.

It felt to me at the time that we, as leaders, were quick to give birth to a child (Living Waters Church), and as parents, we all vowed before God to look after our baby. But when it became sick we abandoned it, allowed it to die—and the prime responsibility lay at my door. Thus began my long night of the soul. The old rejection problem suffered at the hands of my father slithered back into my life like the wily serpent that stalks its prey. Despite the fact that I still pastored a small flock, it became difficult to hold onto my initial vision of church planting. The sudden downward trend in membership, enforced by the accusations of my peers who appeared to see me as the problem, along with the financial losses incurred, all served to undermine the initial faith I started out with. I almost began to believe that evil could not be overcome by good. A time of second-guessing and self-deprecation took place, but in the midst of all this, the ministry still took preeminence, as it always did.

The Bigger Picture

Another problem I faced came from a medication prescribed for depression by my doctor, years earlier, when Adeline and I grappled with the aftermath of the business loss and initial establishment of Living Waters Church. At the time, the problems of attrition in my insurance business plagued my thoughts. In December of 2000, my bank account stood at $4,000.00, commissions from sales made in the second half of that year, which provided enough security for us to take a ten-day vacation in the United States. On our return to Canada, I checked my bank statement and discovered a nasty surprise; the cancellation of almost one hundred percent of the insurance sold in the final months of 2000. This left me with a negative income to start the new year with. At the time, my health started to deteriorate to the point where I could not sleep at night, and dark insidious thoughts invaded my mind. My doctor prescribed an anti-depressant as the solution. The new medication worked wonders, and I perked up to the point where my life became stable again.

The anti-depressant, however, presented a double-edged sword. In the beginning, life appeared worth living, and I found my old self again; but this began to change over time. After a few years of being on the medication, I discovered that no highs or lows existed in my daily emotional regime. Everything appeared to be on the level, which may seem to be ideal—but in fact is a form of false peace. We have emotions for a reason, and when they are removed, there is no longer a useful measure of accountability. The end of the world would not have evoked any concern and a subtle intrusion of indifference crept into my decisions when faced by any form of adversity. The walkout by the music group in late 2005, however, started me on a spiral back to depression, so I sought an increase in the amount of anti-depressant taken to offset this latest development.

With little desire to be on unemployment insurance for too long, I made every effort to find a job to supplement our income; but difficult times reigned, and my age waged war on the few opportunities that cropped up. A commercial on television, that advertised a network marketing business caught Adeline's eye one day, and she suggested I make contact with the company to find out if it may be a viable sort of operation for me.

I made the contact, listened to the hype and gush of accolades that surround these types of businesses and decided it might be worth a try. I didn't have any money for an investment; but my American supervisor encouraged a step of faith in the use of my credit card. He maintained that most people didn't have the necessary investment to start with and that the debt incurred would soon be paid off by the sales of their product. The health food giant, registered in the United States, made all sorts of promises and overtures of potential sales and profitability, but in the end these turned out to be false. Desperation moved me past my better judgment, and so a dance with multi-level-marketing began in earnest. I registered a business for the

The Bigger Picture

purpose of tax legality, and also to facilitate the deposits of all the dollars about to be earned.

My up-line, a man by the name of Joseph, schooled me in the operation of my new business venture and all our lengthy discussions racked up large telephone bills. I will say that almost all MLM businesses are a rip-off. Everyone else seems to get rich except you. Any money made off sales paled into insignificance against the costs of the leads which I purchased from the company. My medication, however, kept me in a state of relaxed carelessness, and it never occurred to me that I wouldn't make money. After four months, however, I took a long look at my business' balance sheet and the shock, although low-key because of the medication, raised my level of concern. My business languished in a deep hole of credit card debt to the tune of $35,000 USD, which at that point included the previous debt incurred on behalf of the church's back rent. Adeline, who left it all up to me, almost suffered a heart attack when I mentioned one morning that my company debt exceeded my income from sales. The strange thing is that I didn't really care if we made it or not; an attitude void of any real sense.

We both realized that my outlook stemmed from the medication. In some ways, I can be quite pragmatic about decisions; and without any real thought, I decided to quit the anti-depressants, cold turkey. I never consulted my doctor about it; I just did it. The results of doing this were twofold: my psyche took a dive into a depression far worse than anything experienced in the past. I also started to get "zinging" brain-sounds in my ears, a periodic rushing of mind sensitivity that would not go away. But through all of it, I understood the financial plight with renewed clarity and my beleaguered mind informed me that something radical needed to be done to save us from financial oblivion. My debt, spread over four credit cards, made continuous payments difficult but minimum payments kept the wolf from the door. One consolation to all this came through Adeline's job with a local financial planner and investment advisor. Another entrepreneur purchased the business, kept Adeline on and promoted her to office manager, with a substantial increase in wages.

The new owner turned out to be an exceptionally good boss, who appreciated the work Adeline did and rewarded her for it. This, to some extent, saved our bacon; but because I could not find a job, we continued to live on a tight budget until a summer job at the local fish cannery came up.

I am extremely thankful for my wonderful wife. She could have blamed me for the predicament, even considered a divorce, as I was not the easiest person to live with over that period of time. The church carried on with the faithful few members who still believed in me as their pastor, but I began to recognize the death-throes of my ministerial career. I consulted with my pastor in Saskatchewan, and set a time when I would step down from pastorship. Pastor Glen assured me that in the matter of the walk-out and the accusations made by the music group, I carried no blame in his eyes. We tried to justify reasons as to why the Creator allowed such goings-on, but nothing could convince me that God still retained an interest in Living Waters Church.

In June of 2007, I resigned my position as pastor, and two of the existing brethren, who felt it an opportunity for them to get into ministry, took over the work. They changed the church's name and one of the two, with previous ministry experience, took over as the interim pastor. I felt tired, defeated, and bereft of almost everything that mattered to me. Adeline mentioned that through all our years of church involvement, she came to hate the bondage that organized religion placed on its adherents. In the wake of my resignation and for a period of several months I walked through the valley of the shadow of death; my reaction to a complete loss of identity.

Colin Setterfield

35: Reflection on a Past Event

A dark place in the life of a faithful person is a time when faith itself comes under scrutiny. Stepping away from what I believed to be my calling in life allowed time for introspection and review of my almost four-decade dance with "the faith." The many positive things that took place over the years now seemed vague—events interpreted as God's blessing on my life and ministry. I looked back on the path which led to our salvation, and recalled the move from the city of Durban to the interior, a small town in Northern Natal, South Africa, where Adeline and I started the swimming pool business, part of our life story mentioned in Chapter 2 of this manuscript. I left some of the details for this chapter.

On a personal level, several years of work invested in a large swimming pool manufacturer prior to the move, provided me with a good knowledge of the industry's construction methods, however, I knew little about the financial and business end of things. Due to the slow economy at the time, it became difficult for people to get loans for such big-ticket items. The first, and only, pool I built belonged to the local optometrist. A few days after the start of construction, the rains came; and, much to my chagrin, flooded everything out. Few people possessed adequate savings in those days, which meant that a credit card provided the financial base for our business. Adeline and I moved into her sister and brother-in-law's home in the wake of their departure to start a new branch of their business in another area. Adeline's brother-in-law, George, made a promise of income for my oversight of a construction team left behind, with equipment and two contracts, to build farm dams. I spent two weeks with him before he left in order to learn the dam-building business, but on his arrival in their new area something happened that caused him to withdraw the offer, so the avenue of income intended for me never came to fruition.

Undeterred, I plunged head-on into building my first pool with the hope that it would be completed in two weeks; but the rains set us back a whole month. Up to this point, Adeline remained in Durban in order to work out the notice she gave to her employer. She, accompanied by my daughter Alison (still a toddler at the time), would travel up every second weekend to be with me. When we were able to get back to construction work, I arranged for a friend in the Durban-based pool business to spend the weekend with us. My friend, accompanied by his wife, hitched a ride with Adeline, and planned to return with her on the Sunday afternoon after the completion of the pool base, not the usual gunnite construction but a concrete-pour procedure. Everything went well with the initial work on the base, and by

Colin Setterfield

Sunday afternoon, my friend and I finalized the main part of the pool structure. To my surprise, Adeline came to me and said she felt anxious about the drive back to Durban.

"Something bad is going to happen and I'm scared," she said.

I told her not to worry about it, and when the time came for them to leave, I breathed a short prayer of God's protection over the vehicle and its occupants.

Half an hour later the police drove their vehicle into the driveway and parked. A police sergeant and his sidekick walked around to the back of the premises to find me.

"Mr. Setterfield? I have come to tell you that your wife and her passengers have been involved in an accident about ten kilometers outside the town."

My heart skipped a beat. "An accident? Are they okay? What happened?"

The sergeant smiled. "They hit a cow, but everyone is fine. Your car has sustained some damage, though. They're waiting there for you to pick them up. Your wife says you have a truck."

I thought back to the moments before Adeline drove away and the memory of her premonition came to mind. I shouted to one of the workers to complete the cleanup, jumped into my truck, and rushed off to the scene of the accident. On arrival, I found Adeline and our friends in conversation with a group of curious bystanders. The car stood on the verge of the road, with

The Bigger Picture

a neat hole through the windshield, made by the hapless cow's horn as it passed over the verge-side of the car's roof, to end up in the long grass. I embraced my traumatized wife and child, thankful for their safety.

My friend's partner, due to start a new job the next morning, left us with no option than for me to drive everyone back to Durban in my truck. The truck's front seat accommodated all four adults with a tight squeeze and with little Alison on her mother's lap, we set off on our journey. To make matters worse the heavens opened, to offload a deluge of rain, which placed a limit on visibility. An hour later, the line of cars in front of us began to slow and then stopped for some unseen obstacle; we could do nothing but sit tight and wait. A police officer, with flashlight in hand, could be seen walking up the line of vehicles toward us and as he drew level with my truck, I rolled down the window to make an enquiry.

"Good evening officer. What appears to be the problem," I asked.

He focussed the flashlight on us. "A creek has flooded the road because of all this rain, and no one can cross over at the moment."

"How long do you think we'll have to wait, Officer?"

The policemen hesitated and looked up at the heavens. "It could be as long as three or four hours," he said. Without another word he moved along to the vehicle behind us.

I cast a quick glance at the looks of disappointment on the faces of my passengers. The dash clock showed the time to be midnight and I made a rough calculation.

"If we can get away by three a.m. we should make Durban by six in the morning," I said.

Three hours later, almost to the second, the first vehicle in line negotiated the water hazard, and the rest followed to the safety of the other side; we reached Durban at sunrise, dropped off our friends and made our way to my mother-in-law's flat. After a quick cleanup and breakfast, Adeline went off to work while I endeavored to get some shuteye before the three-hour trip back home.

Much later that afternoon, after a long, boring drive, I parked in the optometrists' driveway and walked around to the backyard to check on the construction site. The client told me the workers all arrived earlier that morning to start work but without me to give the instructions they left again. I threw up my hands in despair and headed for home in desperate need of sleep.

The next day, I discovered that the concrete mixer, a large industrial model rented from the local equipment rental company, still contained a half-load of mix from the previous day's work. This presented a huge problem. The moments that followed the arrival of the police on site blurred into a jumble of confused actions and I did not have a clear recollection of the instructions given to my workforce at the time. When the rental company arrived to remove the mixer, the driver hitched the machine to his truck and left. I knew he would be back.

Ten minutes later he returned. "Mr. Setterfield! Why didn't you clean out the drum? It's ruined. We'll have to charge you for a replacement."

This would destroy any hopes of making a profit on the pool. I explained the details with regard to the accident and the man nodded his head in sympathy.

"You had better come in and talk to the boss," he said.

The company's owner also showed a measure of empathy. He knew Adeline's brother-in-law, George, personally and I could see he wanted to give me a break.

"I should really get this drum replaced, but I will make a concession," he said. "If you are prepared to spend time with a jackhammer, it may be possible to remove the hardened concrete, but you will have to be extremely careful not to puncture the drum."

There seemed no other way out for me. "I'll do it. Thanks for being so understanding," I said.

Colin Setterfield

After about eleven hours of work with the jackhammer my fingers felt numb and tattered, my ears rang like Big Ben, and my nose, hair, and eyes all clogged up with fine dust, but I soldiered on. At 12:30 a.m. the next morning I managed to clear the last remnants of concrete from the drum.

Back at home, I sat in the bathtub and tried to make sense of everything. To add to my dilemma, the hot-water tank element burned out, so I had to make do with cold water for my cleanup. Needless to say, my spirit dropped to its lowest level. Exhaustion, disillusionment, and defeat surrounded me. The pool construction business appeared to be at a standstill; my beautiful car, a Triumph 2000 station wagon, languished in a local scrapyard and awaited the insurance company's adjuster. Dark thoughts of suicide entered my mind for a brief moment but I knew such a dire action would not solve anything. I couldn't run away. My lovely, faithful wife and an eighteen-month-old baby girl still needed me. I cried out to God for help.

As I sat there in the cold water a feeling, like a gust of warm air, flowed over my body and a sudden peace filled my heart.

I am amazed what the mind can make one believe when the chips are down. In my experience, there have been very few people who can testify to the fact that they woke up one day and decided to know God better. In most circumstances this type of consideration is made under duress. A few days later, Godfrey and Olivia invited me to the Word of God church, which became our first spiritual home. Any good fundamental, evangelical believer will posit that all these tribulations are the result of a benevolent God who sought to save my soul and bring me to the point of accepting Him into my life. I used to make a big issue about how God led me out of the darkness and into the light, however, over time, it became clear that the Infinite Creator has designed another law for the purpose of real-time results: the law of probability. I will explain.

Our humanity places us at a distinct disadvantage in our relationship with the world. We are not born self-sufficient, as some animals in the wild are. Our parents needed to protect and nurture us until we could fend for ourselves because the world, in general, is hostile to our wellbeing. The idea of a God who looks after us, and provides for our needs is a highly desirable concept, one most people will accept without prejudice. It is more likely in moments when we have come to the end of our wits and efforts to protect our interests that we seriously consider this God whom the Bible speaks of as one who will become a protector and keeper. It is in our nature to seek a power greater than ourselves when faced with situations that might overwhelm us.

This thought began to make me consider all the positives and negatives that have taken place in my own life. Not every prayer for my wellbeing, or that of my property, have ever been answered in a way that assured me of God's protection in every occasion. In fact, negative circumstances outweigh the positives in most everyone's lives. Does this mean that God only answers some of the time, or that He has some sort of spiritual algorithm that decides how He will respond? I believe the writers of scripture have led us down the rabbit hole in their desire to make the Biblical God so benevolent toward us that we believe we are completely taken care of. The whole thrust of spiritual teaching is the "personal relationship" we have with Christ; He is our personal savior, our confidant, and most intimate friend. We are able to enter this type of relationship with God through the wooing of the Holy Spirit, under the premise that when we give our lives over to Him, He enters our beings and we are filled with light and power. This is the dualist concept—that before we met Christ, we did not have God in our lives, and we existed as a part of the darkness that is the world system. Little wonder that we misconstrue the way things really work.

In the previous chapter, I explained what happened near the end of my ministry and how I couldn't reconcile God's lack of action when everything around me crashed. I knew the commitment in my own heart, and I know I gave God four decades of my unwavering faithfulness. Even a heartless, earthly ruler would not treat his subjects with such disdain. Did God just decide one day that I no longer fitted the bill? I don't think so. There is a reason why certain things pass muster and others don't.

The Bigger Picture

*

Before I continue with what happened after my resignation from the church. I want to share a theory called the "DR Theory."

36: DR Theory

I know from my own experience that fundamental believers struggle with any concept outside the normal Christian belief system—and DR Theory is just that. In order to understand this hypothesis, it will be necessary to think outside of the biblical box.

Decision/Reality theory suggests that your decisions create your realities. While certain realities just appear in our lives without a plausible reason it is a fact that much of our reality is as a result of a conscious decision we have made. For instance: No one chooses to get cancer or any other type of debilitating disease but there are situations where I make a decision and that decision brings me into a new set of circumstances. One of the more speculative approaches to Quantum Physics is biocentrism,[36] which suggests that universal matter, in the form of a wave function, responds to observation by the mind; when the wave function is observed, it collapses into what we perceive as a material form or the construction of a reality. The book Biocentrism, by Dr. Robert Lanza, is groundbreaking science at its best, and the ultimate suggestion here is that consciousness is the creator of reality. This is a difficult concept to grasp, but one

The Bigger Picture

could say that it is life that creates the universe, and not the other way round. The view that spacetime is a wave of probability (particles that are really forms of energy in an entangled state with one another), and awaits the function of consciousness to bring the expression of reality to the mind may appear to be a statement of science fiction. The possible truth in this suggestion, however, confirms the mystery factor of quantum physics. It has been said that anyone who believes they understand the quantum world is a liar.

I have mentioned the hypothesis of biocentrism because it lends much credence to the DR theory, in that if we are creating reality from a wave of probability, then it is possible there might also be encoded into that same wave function an infinite set of possibilities that respond to the decisions we make. This is how it might work: Every person follows a critical path through the realms of spacetime, from the time they are born to the time they die. Over the period of the incarnation (spirit/soul in human flesh), I suggest that we not only create reality from observation through our consciousness, but we also create a path through spacetime by means of the decisions we make (or decisions made on our behalf).

Take, for instance, a scenario where I wake up in the morning, go about my ablutions and breakfast, and then make a decision to leave my home at a certain time. I drive down to the crossroad, which has a set of traffic lights; and as things go, if I leave at the same time every day, the traffic light will be (let's say) red. I spend about two minutes at the intersection before it turns green and I go on my way. If I decide to leave ten minutes later than normal, the events at that traffic light might be different. It may be green for me to go, but it also allows for a different possibility to come into play, because a bus has left at its normal time and is barreling down toward the same intersection. Then the unthinkable happens; the bus' brakes fail at the moment of its approach as I enter the intersection. Bang! I end up in hospital. Why did this happen? Because I decided to change the timing of a normal event by staying ten minutes longer at home on that particular morning.

I posit that my decision to do so changed my position physically, and opened up one of the many possibilities that are pre-programmed into spacetime. This may seem an over-simplification of an action related to an event, but it makes sense that my decision created a new reality for me. Had I left at the normal time, the usual outcome would have been more likely, and I would have arrive at my work in one piece. Sometimes it's not my decision that changes the range of possibilities; it could be a decision made by someone else, and which brings them into my area of spacetime, but then again I would have made a conscious decision to leave at the normal time, so it comes back to the same thing: my decision still brought me into the realm of someone else's spacetime continuum.[37]

The Bigger Picture

Why am I making this point? If there is any truth in this theory, then the infinite Creator has no need to interfere in our daily problems. It is the law of probability that takes over and renders the result. God, in creative genius, has already "programmed" all possible events into spacetime, and He would therefore not need to intervene to change any physical outcome which comes about as the result of a human decision. This is why we have good things and bad things happen to us on our journey, despite fervent prayers for protection. It also explains why bad things sometimes happen to good people, or why the innocent suffer the consequences of other's decisions. Am I saying that God has created the world, and He now sits back and just watches? Not at all. I believe the Infinite One indwells each and every human being in the form of consciousness which extends past the divine and enters our personal world, but not to directly influence or intervene in our thoughts, which would be a violation of our personal will. As previously alluded to I contend that God is present in every person in the form of a higher self (a God-self which still relates to me as "myself"), and in the form of a lower self, which is predominantly my mind. The lower self-creates the impression that I am separate from everyone else, a necessary provision for us to interact with the external world. We are all, however, connected through the divine consciousness, which also makes us a part of the universe itself. The universe is a living entity, an extension of the divine essence that lurks within the quantum wave function, and facilitates the collapse of that function into material forms when observed by the human mind.

The presence of the "higher self" will provide each of us with the wisdom we need to make the best decisions if we know how to access it. This higher self (God's consciousness), knows the path ahead with all the resultant possibilities, and has made this provision available to us so that we may seek the higher self's wisdom before we make decisions that move us forward into the infinite sea of probability. We do not need to look outside of ourselves for this wisdom, for it is within. The higher self will also give us access to the "collective consciousness" of all other beings, or groups, which through prayer and collaborative consultation are focused on something specific. To support this concept, there has been much research on a subject called "morphic resonance" conducted by the well-known biologist, Rupert Sheldrake, who has provided proof of a "collective memory" common to most species.

The common attitude amongst fundamental evangelicals is that we pray for God's protection over our situations, but our protection actually lies in good decisions made under the auspice of the higher self. The Creator has made every provision through the establishment of "probable outcomes" already programmed into spacetime, and we should all be able to access the wisdom available for guidance and protection. There is nothing

The Bigger Picture

wrong in a personal prayer for a good outcome, but we first need to seek the wisdom for whatever decision is about to be made. *You should do whatever your conscience is telling you, but information is available through a meditative process; and if you can access it, the outcome will be far more concrete than anything a general prayer will provide.

The dualist mentality subtly perceives God as being separate from our souls and we need therefore need to find our wisdom outside of ourselves. The scriptures, however, teach us that we are "one with God," but we seem to comprehend this as something that pertains to a mutual consensus of ideology. We fail to take the word "indwelling" at its base meaning: inside of us, integrated entirely with our being. The false perception of dualism came to the West during the Reformation period, out of which Protestantism sprung, to impose a whole new regime on believers. From it, we understood that we must be "born again" of the Spirit of God, otherwise we are not "saved" and will not be able to be with God in heaven. This concept gave rise to a perception that there are those who do not possess the Spirit of God, and who will spend their eternity in a place called Hell. The erroneous conclusion is that we need to "receive" something we already all have: the Creator's presence within us. Different versions of this ritual have been imposed on the church for "joining our spirits with God," and this led to the establishment of the many denominations we see in the world today.

Fundamentalism in its worst form will cut off anyone who does not adhere to the "faith" expounded by religious predecessors, an attitude resultant in many wars, deaths, and hypocritical nonsense over the years of human history. Much of the religious teachings have caused a perceived separation between the "heathen" and the "child of God." I doubt whether Jesus ever intended that polarized groups should become the instrument of God's witness to the world. In Matthew 10:35, Jesus tells his disciples that he had come to "set sons against fathers and daughters against mothers," but the truth behind this saying is that he knew the human heart well enough to predict this type of behavior. He knew his message would stir up the opinion polls of human nature, but I don't believe Jesus ever intended it to bring division.

*

In the next chapter, I return to finish off the story of my ministerial career, so we can delve deeper into this bigger picture to which I have referred to on numerous occasions.

37: The End of a Long Road

My resignation from Living Waters Church brought a long-term, full-time ministry to an end. While I still clung to the fundamental hem of Jesus's garment, a distinct shift of awareness started to take place in my thoughts and in June 2007, thirty-five years of dedicated service in God's Kingdom came to an end.

My fundamentalist mindset taught me that God held me in the palm of His hand, and as one of His servants, provision to prosper would always be a part of the deal. My dream, however, wrapped up in the pursuit of the Kingdom, lay shattered at my feet. At the age of sixty-three years, retirement stared me in the face, with a measure of financial debt as the consolation.

For several weeks I fought off depression and took long walks to clear my mind. Pastor Glen wrote me a long letter of encouragement. He mentioned that a retired Calgary-based couple, members of the denominational fellowship to which we subscribed, now lived on the Island and hoped to start a meeting in their home. Pastor Glen thought this small, non-denominational fellowship might be a good way for Adeline and I to heal our wounds. He explained that they did not intend to start another church, but rather to provide a service for hurt and weary believers. Adeline and I tried a few of the other local churches, but once you have been in leadership, it is very difficult to settle down under a new regime with a leader you don't know. On top of that, I could no longer trust my life into the hands of the organized church.

All the negative experiences in my relationships came to the fore, and I found it easier to withdraw from the company of others. These innocuous, dark thoughts took over my life and I decided to keep everyone at arm's length, where they couldn't hurt me.

We did, however, take Pastor Glenn up on his offer of an introduction to the couple with the home fellowship. I wasn't ready to walk away from church life altogether, so we visited and started to fellowship with their small group. The home fellowship did not operate under a leader who directed matters, but provided the softer approach of facilitation by the homeowners. We started with worship and gravitated into discussions about Christ and the Bible. The wife of the facilitating couple played the piano, and asked me to accompany her on my guitar during the worship periods, a true blessing for my fragmented attitude toward spiritual matters at the time. The spiritual disconnect created within me a desire to research everything ever learned about Christianity over the years. My ministry overshadowed everything else in life—with all my eggs placed in one basket there appeared little opportunity for a new direction. How could it have gone so wrong, unless I sabotaged it all myself?

It will always be speculated upon by less discerning believers who believe sin to be the cause of one's adversity and the reason for failure... but Christians agree that we are all sinners, be it sinners saved by grace. I spent hours on my walks in an attempt to pin my failure on sins of the past, sins of thought, sins of omission, transgressions against standing authorities, etc., but nothing provided enough conviction to count as real reasons for the demise of my ministry. Would an all-loving deity not protect His child when it really mattered? The thought that we may have some deep misconceptions about the God of the Bible entered my thinking for the first time, a notion which initially sent me on a guilt trip, because Christians should never question the veracity of the Word of God.

To the Christian fundamentalist, the Bible is an inerrant work of perfection and above suspicion of error. In the academic pursuits that pertained to my personal ministerial career, the polemical studies always started and ended with a strong Christian bias, focused on discouragement of any alternative research into matters with regard to the authenticity of actual events. The real existence of characters in the course of history, as seen from a secular point of view, is not acceptable in the realm of Christian academia, who see most of what the secular historians come up with as disinformation.

Colin Setterfield

I made a decision to consider the works of those who made it their mission to expose all the inconsistencies, plus provide plausible proof of the many misinterpreted passages and words as written in the original Hebrew and Greek languages; but these issues will not be dealt with here, because there are enough extant works available for factual confirmation. When focused on such a work, be sure to do your own research into the sources provided, because it is too easy to accept what others with a vendetta might say on a subject of interest. It took me a long time to work through everything necessary in my quest for an informed decision.

One possible reason why many religious people reject any new and emergent hypotheses with regard to our origins and evolution is couched in the premise that the Creator could only have created the universe exactly as the book of Genesis portrays it. And I must conclude that God did just that. The language of Genesis, however, allows only for basic terms of reference:

"In the beginning, God created the heavens and the Earth..."; Genesis 1:1. The word "created" is a very generic expression for anything that is made, be it in ancient or modern terms. Our first impression is that of a deity, perhaps in human-like form, who constructed the Earth with both hands, or as Genesis puts it: God "spoke" things into existence, an apt metaphoric statement to imply the impression of forming something out of nothing. But the Creator is not somewhere up in space, molding things with human-like hands; our deductions, based on the proof of an evolutionary process innate in nature since the beginning of our planet, is blatant and consistent with the concept to "create." So, why could this not have been the reality behind the metaphor? In my humble opinion, a form of evolution—or any other means of creation, if there be material proof for it—is how God could have set things in motion. I found a work by Michael Dowd, Thank God for Evolution, to be an amazing possibility for the creation account which, to me, certainly did not disprove God as being the original Creator. Our newer science suggests that Darwin did not have everything sewn up, and I see the possibility for interventions by other god-created life forms in the universe; it's a big place!

My belief in a "creative being" is based mostly on causality; **38** our world, made up of physical matter that defaults out of the quantum wave under observation, is a salient point of the "beginnings" and "endings" one would expect from the process of universal entropy. Anything with a beginning begs need of a creative process to be set in motion by a creative force. We can go on a mission to discover "who created what" and "what came first," but there is no viable answer to be derived from what preceded our universe. We have hypotheses of multiple or parallel universes, but none of these are ends in themselves. Religious minds look for a definitive answer as the hook upon which they may hang their religious hats, and a creative, higher power is what fits the bill. It brings a hope of eternal life: a position in which we will always have life, not in human form, but in a metaphysical or spiritual sense. It is everyone's choice to accept this position, or continue to live without an answer.

I realize I'm a bit of dreamer, but for me, it is preferable to extend my faith into the realm of possibilities to which both scripture and science allude. This explains my love for science fiction and why most of the fiction books I have written explore the possibilities of space travel and the discovery of life on other planets. It is a gift that has allowed me to see life through different eyes, a provision in the wiring of my brain that has graciously afforded me a glimpse of the Bigger Picture.

I no longer see those instrumental in bringing my ministry to a close as the enemies of my soul (which I did at first), but I applaud them as unwitting heroes who placed me in a position to think more deeply about spiritual matters, and thus open a whole new world for me. If you ask whether I believe everything I've researched about this Bigger Picture, I would say that "belief" is a very strong word; I do, however, entertain the possibilities of the ideas expressed by many of the authors who have walked along this thought-provoked path. I once believed (as many still do) in a literal devil, and that all conspiracy theories were authored by him; but I soon realized a certain amount of

The Bigger Picture

these theories held elements of truth, not to be rejected out of hand.

In the next few chapters, I will share how some of these possibilities support the Bigger Picture, and why. You may have to fasten your seatbelt though, because much of what I bring to the table may test your present belief system to the core. The haters are out there, uninformed people who will have much to say about this evolving picture, so do your best to keep an open mind. There are things afoot in the present that may change the understanding of our origins as we know them.

Colin Setterfield

38: Entertaining the Possibilities of the Bigger Picture

The answer to the question of a "bigger picture" with regard to our origins and evolution is still in the process of being revealed. We are in a state of transition. Soon the governments of the world powers will come clean about phenomena that have recently occurred during the Cold War, and have occurred repeatedly throughout the history of civilization. At this point, the superstructure of the Bigger Picture is in place. This allows us to build the final pieces out of several possibilities available in the form of certain salient theories which scream at us through the many testimonies of insiders and relevant internet sites. Some of these theories are pure conjecture, while others hold water. It is only a matter of time before we will be able to build the final stage of this viewpoint. When this happens, contention between the war-mongers and peace advocates will be brought to a head, religions will find a new perspective, and the end of reliance on fossil fuels will be in sight. We may even be able to move toward a new economic system which will benefit everyone on the planet and not enslave them.

The Bigger Picture

It is time for the average citizen of the world to know that we are not alone in this universe. The subject over which there has been so much speculation and debate is none other than the question of UFOs and extraterrestrial life.

Are we really being visited by Extraterrestrials, and is there any possibility that our origins might have had an alien involvement?

The discussion of possible life elsewhere in the universe is a household subject. The question of extraterrestrial craft sightings and whether or not we are alone in the universe has raised suspicions about a worldwide government cover-up of the real answers to the UFO phenomenon. A host of opinions have inundated the world of literature and film under the guise of entertainment, or conspiracy theory, which until more recently gained little momentum. The advent of the Hubble Space Telescope, however, supplemented by the discoveries of thousands of exoplanets,[39] created a tsunami of interest with regard to the Cosmos. This unbound enthusiasm for outer-space truth soon led to the establishment of TV channels and websites dedicated to the question of our cohabitation with other possible life-forms in the universe. The support of UFO phenomenology soared after the turn of the last century with the emergence of whistleblowers involved in unacknowledged secret space programs, organized and run by a shadow government called the Cabal. This cabal, made up of certain elite and wealthy members of society, managed all UFO sightings, abductions and crashed spacecraft through famous projects like "Sign", "Grudge", and "Bluebook", in an effort to debunk the experiences because it feared widespread paranoia. But this is not the only reason for the coverup. A host of new technologies, discovered from reverse-engineered extraterrestrial craft, have led to secretive government black op programs and a cache of weapon development projects for the military-industrial complex.

Polls show that while many still remain skeptical about UFO's, aliens, and coverup programs, a greater number of people now believe that where there is smoke there is fire. The sheer multitude of more than 100 billion stars in our own galaxy, many with exoplanets, is a positive indicator that life similar to ours exists in the huge conglomerate. The famous equation conceived by Dr. Frank Drake in 1961, for the stimulation of scientific dialogue at the first Green Bank SETI meeting, shows that more than 4,500 civilizations could exist in our Milky Way galaxy alone. The number offered by the equation may seem to be overstated but it does have a scientific base and can serve as an indicator. Visitation to distant parts of the universe is thought by many to be an impossible quest for humanity due to the lack of technology in propulsion systems, but in recent times new

The Bigger Picture

ideas have come to light; like the "quantum link in spacetime"[40] theory and the move toward consciousness,[41] both which are key to the future of space travel. What the mainstream scientific community declares as pseudoscience is, in many respects, on the brink of elevation to the top rank and file of the propulsion industry's discipline.

There is a trepidatious attitude toward the expected changes, but they are inevitable. History books will be rewritten or supplemented; mainline academics will re-school themselves on new sciences that they once outlawed, and the energy sector will be managed in a move away from fossil fuels to cleaner alternatives. Within a few years, the world as we know it is going to be quite different: all poverty could be eradicated when free energy from the quantum vacuum[42] is made available to all. This will more than likely not be a smooth transition. Sicknesses and diseases will eventually be eradicated with a flood of new medical technologies learned from extraterrestrial sources. I know this sounds like science fiction, but the cards have already been dealt, and partial disclosures have made their way into the mainstream of society through a process of whistleblowing and fringe journalism.

The cover-up by military establishments started in earnest after the second world war. It began with the famous UFO crash on a ranch close to the town of Roswell, New Mexico, USA. A host of sightings over many of the nuclear facilities in the US,

UK, and Russia created enough concerns for the governments involved to develop a mindset of paranoia which has become responsible for keeping the public in the dark about extraterrestrial visitations. The authorities demonized any mainstream scientist who supported the presence of UFOs and treated whistleblowers as enemies of the state. Sworn to secrecy about their experiences many military whistleblowers waited for up to fifty years or longer before they started to trickle forward and make their stories known. The Sirius Disclosure Project started in 1993 by Dr. Steven Greer, author of the number one iTunes bestseller "Unacknowledged", has gone a long way to force the secrets out into the open. Organizations like MUFON, a non-profit that investigates extraterrestrial sightings, plus YouTube, Gaia and Collective Evolution (global digital video streaming services), have brought the matter fully into the public eye, with thousands of videos on the subject of UFOs and extraterrestrial contacts. Of course, not all that one views or listens to is credible, but the charlatans are soon exposed. For the subject to suffer continued redaction by governments is for them a lost cause as the Internet cannot be bridled. Pandora's Box is open.

There is a concerted effort to create disinformation by the warmongering governments and weapon-producing military industrial complex, who don't want the truth about their black op and secret space programs to be known. The famous German scientist, Werner von Braun, declared on his deathbed that the

U.S. Government will try to create a threat with regard to a coming alien invasion. They will attempt to motivate the industrialized countries of the Earth to weaponize our solar system and thereby keep the world in a state of war, a move that will benefit their long-term intentions to make billions of dollars and control the masses.

There is no truth in an alien threat to our planet. The extraterrestrials who buzzed the nuclear facilities after World War Two and who watched our progress with weapons of mass destruction, only have the Earth's best interests at heart. Sometimes the truth is stranger than fiction. The extraterrestrials have maintained a presence to make sure we do not blow ourselves to pieces or destroy the environment. We know that the military industrial complex[43] has been able to reverse engineer downed UFOs, and have constructed very realistic flying saucers which are the ones to be used in a campaign of disinformation with regard to the evil intentions of extraterrestrials. Many of the cattle mutilation and abduction cases have been proved to be the subject of this campaign. Seasoned ufologists have often warned enthusiasts not to be misled by this effort at disinformation. The genuine saucers we might see will be those that can appear and disappear within nanoseconds as they emerge into, or leave our dimension. The government craft used in the disinformation project, although endowed with UFO back-engineered technology are ships manufactured by the military industrial complex.

Several channeling groups have confirmed the existence of extraterrestrials called The Guardians, who are in fact looking after our interests and are keen that over a given time, there should be a full disclosure of their presence. There is a benevolent Federation of planets out there (in our galaxy) who wants us to overcome our innate violent natures and join with them in bonafide membership. There are also other aliens who want to manipulate the human race for their own selfish ends, but the Galactic Federation is keeping them at bay. The Federation's intention is for us to reach a status of the highest technological advancement possible, a future that holds peaceful living and disease-free conditions plus interstellar space travel. Many of these federation members have millions of years of evolution behind them, and are far more advanced than we are. They want to help us maximize our consciousness abilities in order for us to reach the highest state of our being that we can aspire to.

It is possible that John Ball's theory, the "Zoo Hypothesis," a cosmic project in which we are being allowed to conform to our own evolutionary path without interference from outside, is the real sum of things until the human race is ready for integration with the rest of the galaxy's creatures. Some authorities feel that we did not evolve here on Earth and that alien masters brought us here and interbred us with the ancient hominids. When we have a good look at the different racial profiles of human society, their features, skin color, and physiques, it is easy to support such a theory. The "Prison Hypothesis" is yet another possibility that assumes humans did not evolve on the Earth. This possibility gets credence from the violent, selfish attitude that is inherent in Homo sapiens. Maybe the Alien Masters removed humans from another planet for incarceration on the Earth, in the hope that time would improve our demeanor.

At this point, we don't know which of these hypotheses might be true, or if there be some other explanations. If the human's compatibility with the Earth's natural bio-physical environment is considered in contrast to the animals that evolved here, a solid case can be made for any of the above scenarios as opposed to the mainstream evolutionary viewpoint. Humans appear to be ill-adapted for the harshness of the seasons and the sun's radiation, which may be a strong indication we did not evolve here. The environment on our original home planet may have been better suited for our survival, in terms of a stable temperature and radiation level.

It doesn't matter which of these theories proves to be true. The intervention by extraterrestrials gives us an extra tier of evolution between the infinite Creator and human beings, which means there is no reason to doubt the existence of a higher cosmic intelligent power for our Genesis. The universe could be full of life similar to Homo sapiens, and also diverse forms that evolve in accordance with their planet's conditions. Every believer can complete the framework for their bigger picture with intervention knowledge, in the understanding that contact with extraterrestrials is a real live fact and brings with it some exciting possibilities that we will discuss in the next chapter.

39: Considering the Possibilities

This chapter may test religious sentiments, and it is to be understood that I present the content here as one of those "possibilities" to be considered in the construction of the bigger picture. Most opinions on the subject of metaphysics vary, and are based on one's philosophical leanings; but all that is required is to have an open mind. It is unfortunate that fundamental religion has demonized the practice of psychic powers that focus on remote viewing, lucid dreaming, psychic contact, and channeling. These gifts have been denounced by well-meaning ministers of the Gospel as lies from the occult, or New Age; but not everything relegated to these disciplines is evil. As a good Christian, I always distanced myself from these phenomena, because the Christian system required this of me; but once released from that fundamental bondage, I saw how these practices are part of a cosmic communication framework that enrich the soul. Because the ETs operate in a higher vibrational realm, one that relies on telepathic discourse, these practices are better suited for the transfer of information and knowledge to the human mind. The relegation of this "realm" concept to that of a new age heresy by fundamentalists is an attempt to obscure the potential it holds for the evolution of our consciousness.

So, what advantage does the Alien Intervention theory bring to us?

Contact with extraterrestrial life, beings who are in some cases millions of years ahead of us technology-wise, will bring answers we may never even have dreamed of. Several people who claim to have worked within the secretive government black ops programs are now coming forward to share their experiences, and the wave of current disclosures via the Internet leaves the governments involved with little wriggle room. They realize the writing is on the wall for their secrecy. The whistleblowers feel less threatened by the disinformation campaign, and are willingly coming forward with little or no compensation for themselves. This is supplemented by the resolve of a few (not the majority), who have been responsible for administering the threat campaign—those who consider themselves as elite players in the suppression of the truth, but feel it is time for a limited disclosure of our real history.

One of the most interesting accounts about alien contact comes from a group of channelers who claim to be in touch with a society of benevolent ETs who call themselves the Ra (pronounced RAW) group.[44] The Ra is a sixth-density collective social memory complex assembly of extraterrestrials[45] who operate under the charter of the One Infinite Creator, the deity we refer to as God. The charter is called the "Law of One" and, as explained by the group, is not a religion. The principles of the Law of One deal with the mechanics of spiritual evolution of all Beings, and the propagation of values is through consciousness and love. The gist of the teaching is aimed at the preparation of "third-density" Beings (like us) to adopt a "service to others" attitude as opposed to "self-service." The Ra have embraced this principle as a collective and have chosen to be of help to less advanced beings, to bring them into the "light" of the Law of One, and what it means to be in the service of the One Infinite Creator.

Some interesting spiritual parallels can be drawn from the content of this material (the Law of One), as well as an insight into some of the famous historical mysteries of the past. If the Ra group are for real, then the enigma of the Great Pyramids is resolved. According to the Ra, they made contact with the ancient Egyptians, at which time they built the pyramids for the propagation of healing and initiation rites. The problem, however, did not lie with the current pharaoh of the time, but with his priests. The Ra wanted to be seen as "equals and servants," not as gods, but the priests decided to treat them as Deity. This meant that a religion started to propagate amongst the Egyptians, a reaction not appreciated by the Ra, so they decided to leave the Earth and wait for a future time when they could return to rectify the distortion. I will not go into how the Ra built the pyramids, but if the reader is interested, the details can be found in the Law of One material, available at the L/L Institute, online.

A reading of the Law of One will produce many biblical parallels, and one wonders if its contents, along with other myths, weren't perhaps passed down by the ETs to later civilizations, with a trickle-down effect that influenced the Eastern religions and the Hebrew writers of ancient scripture. I realize that critics of the Intervention Hypothesis will maintain that the Ra material is a prefabrication of human channelers' minds, with the Law of One principle being based on biblical texts rather than the other way round. We know, however, that aliens definitely visited the ancient Egyptians, because a host of spaceship/astronaut etchings are depicted in their artwork. One of the most interesting aspects of the Law of One is that it propagates the transmigration of souls.

The Transmigration of Souls

The reader may not be familiar with this term, but it is, in essence, the process of reincarnation—a concept most Christians do not believe in, because it is seen as a doctrine of the Indian religions. The Indian concept includes the incarnation of souls into either human or animal bodies, and remains a strong belief among several religions, namely Hinduism, Jainism, and Buddhism. The prominent Greek philosophers Pythagoras and Plato also both believed the soul to be immortal, and after death could migrate into new bodies. The Catholic Church taught reincarnation until the Council of Constantinople in 553 CE, after which they declared it to be heresy. The history behind its abolishment from the Christian Faith is of some interest, to say the least.

In the second century, the influential historian, Origen of Alexandria, supported and believed in the transmigration of souls, which ensured that the teaching was well ensconced in Christian values before the council took action. The Greek Historian Procopius, noted that the Byzantine Emperor, Justinian (482 - 565 CE), married to an ambitious woman, Theodora, who stopped at nothing to gain power for continued rule, declared the transmigration of souls to be a heretical doctrine. Theodora's apparent cruelty knew no bounds. Her influence over political affairs became well known. Procopius contended that the Empress feared the doctrine of Karma, which goes hand in hand with the cycle of rebirth. She feared it would become the judge of her life's actions, so she influenced her husband to have the interpretation abolished from the church's official teachings. There is also a belief that Jesus spent his early years (age 12-30) in India, and came away with the transmigration of souls as a part of the process of salvation. The earliest mention of reincarnation is as far back as 2600 BCE, which means it could have originated in Egypt through the propagation of the Law of One by the extraterrestrial visitors.

In modern times, several books have been written about children who have been incarnated before and remember their previous lives. The apparent idea behind the transmigration of souls is that each incarnation will help in the improvement of Karmic experience until one reaches a state of bliss. According to the Law of One, you return to the collective after each death in order to plan out your next incarnation for the improvement of service to others. It is your inclusion of "catalyst", or hardships, in future incarnations that will deal with the negative side of your personality and bring your soul to ascension. It is alleged that Good Karma is produced through kindness and compassion for others. It is a concept that makes more sense than an eternal worship session around God's throne. The mind or soul, with its non-local quantum ability, is a facilitation (but not a construction) of the human brain, and it may have its source from within the general quantum wave. The discovery of "tubulin," a substance said to contain quantum properties that exists within the microtubules of the brain's cytoskeleton, may have a correlation with consciousness; but this has not yet been proven. Evident by their desperate attempts to keep any form of metaphysics out of "real" science, mainstream advocates are vehemently opposed to anyone using quantum mechanics in the same sentence as consciousness. No one is allowed to entertain the possibility of a quantum connection or to think outside of the narrow, closed-minded mainstream box. Pseudoscience, however, is on the rise.

Finding a Path Forward

The real question is, where do we go from here? What do we take for ourselves out of all this apparent speculation? How much different is this bigger picture from what ancient scriptures have already revealed to us?

What I have broached in this manuscript is the nuts and bolts of a potential reality about our origin and the cosmic plan for an infinite life. We have learned from ancient scripture that the Creator loves the creation, and is in essence one with it. The search for a greater sense of reality in my belief system did not change what I already believed about eternity. I came to Earth as an eternal being, incarnated into a human form, and will return to the eternal state in a spiritual (or energy) form. The soul does not die when the body dies. If it is true that a cycle of rebirths does occur, there is then a distinct possibility that I might return by means of a future incarnation in another human body to further "work out my salvation." It does not appear that the concept of reincarnation included the soul's return to animals, birds, insects, or any other type of life form, which is a tenet of Hinduism. There is no indication that the early Christians believed incarnations involved anything other than the human form.

A literal interpretation of sacred scripture will limit our personal truth. The reason why the Bible contains all those beautiful metaphorical, allegorical, and symbolic pictures is to induce the human mind to search for the reality hidden within (seek and you will find...). A literal interpretation might suffice for the time periods over which the writers penned the actual descriptions and parallels, but the realities encapsulated will become obscure to successive generations who have to deal with changing times, newer technologies, and divergent cultural values. The Bigger Picture is one that is all-inclusive and includes Cosmic truths (truths pertinent to the entire universe) and not solely human life. We are meant to view our wonderful home planet and the amazing night sky with all of its billions of stars and realize that we, as humans, are an integral part of the whole, not separate entities.

The universe is a living organism that supports human life as agents of free will, who contribute toward its experience of self, because we are intricately connected to everything around us. The celestial bodies contain all the physical elements which form and support human life, but their cycle of life and death is required to make such a propagation. The Bigger Picture is one that includes our planet and the entire cosmos, along with humans and other life forms, for the full expression of our destiny. The Bigger Picture is one you construct for yourself with the understanding that scripture is a road you can only explore in metaphorical terms. Those brave souls who peek outside of the proverbial fundamental box will be in awe with regard to the size of the room that contains the box.

The church, however, still provides a platform for the spiritually like-minded. It can serve as a conduit for the love of the infinite Creator to the world, but the administration of its spiritual principles lies in the hands of fallible people. The ecclesiastical institution seeks to direct the minds of its adherents along the lines of doctrinal leanings, all which are humanly tainted to facilitate a form of control, which will lead to ongoing splits, breakups, and controversies. The subtle seeds of self-destruction, pride, and greed are innate in all human beings. There is no change in our DNA when we have a "born again" experience, because the change of values is based purely on metaphysical terms. It happens in the mind, and will not eradicate these vices other than on a psychic, or moral/thought, level.

The advice of the Apostle Paul is that in order for forgiveness, love, and kindness to gain any traction in the face of betrayals and disappointments brought on us by others, we need to "reckon ourselves to be dead to sin." This is proof that spirituality is all about the state of the mind. Even if the full power of God exists within the higher self, it is still subject to the human element (the lower self) because we possess free will. The power of God is not available to counteract our decision-making, which is the mechanism for creating our personal realities.

40: Back to Secular Life

The home fellowship proved to be a salvation for our battle-weary souls. After years of preaching sermons, I felt ready to sit back and listen to others discuss the pros and cons of life in the spirit. Our host couple provided topical questions to get the discussion going, and everyone chimed in with their opinions. I enjoyed the worship period, because it gave me an opportunity to play along with my guitar. Shortly after we joined the group I managed to find employment as a Warranty Officer with a local RV company, a job I knew little about. I quickly learned the software required for the transmission of warranty work to the various vendors, and started on the three-month backlog of work orders and invoices. The manager told me to take my time, but eager to prove my commitment, I tore into the work and finished the backlog in about four weeks, a gesture that did not go unnoticed. Because of my industrial engineering background, improvements to their existing systems came as a natural course of events; and within three months, I received a significant raise in my wages. Another three months passed in which I applied to all the existing vendors for an increase in our shop rate (the rate charged for work we did under warranty), and managed to make such a good argument that all the vendors agreed to pay the amount applied for. Money for our warranty work began to pour in, which pleased the company's owner so much he granted me another significant wage increase.

For the first time since we arrived in Canada, our financial situation improved enough for us to face life with a greater sense of security; and after we paid off the mortgage on our home, I chipped away at the credit card debt. In 2009, a fortuitous meeting between one of our motorcycle friends and a couple, newly arrived in the city, provided a new opportunity for me to consider. The couple owned a Gold Wing and wanted to ride with folk who knew the area. Their company, a large international construction group that specialized in oil and natural gas refineries, moved the couple from the United States to the Island to oversee a new project, a peak shaving facility to be built on First Nations land in the mountains not far from our city.

Our motorcycle friend invited this couple to join us on a long weekend motorcycle jaunt to the mainland, and they agreed. When Vic and I met, we enjoyed a mutual rapport due to his involvement on a contract in South Africa, my country of birth, a decade prior.

About three weeks later, Vic called me at work and asked if I would have lunch with him. It turned out that he, as the superintendent of the contract, wanted to offer me a job as a material coordinator with their company. He promised there would be other contracts after that in different places, and the pay would be three times what I earned in the RV business. This is a good position to be in when you are sixty-four years old and wondering how it is you will manage to retire with some financial backing. I felt reticent, however, to leave my current job, as it offered me a measure of security and a livable wage; but after speaking with Adeline, and in consideration of the new company's benefits, I decided to take the plunge. The manager of the RV group, disappointed that I chose to leave told me his company would not be able to match the offer but he understood my position. He realized that due to my advanced age the change would help me establish a livable retirement.

On the spiritual front, Adeline and I settled into the home-group fellowship. My shift of spiritual paradigm, by this time well under way became exacerbated by the emersion into a much rougher workforce element. I kept my past history as a minister of religion secret, because I feared it might change the way my peers treated me.

The truth, however, came out; and for the first six months, I pulled the short stick of foul religious jokes combined with as much foul language my coworkers could muster. I almost resigned the position on several occasions, but circumstances started to change when the other two workers in the materials department found out I possessed a lot of wisdom with regard to relationships. As a former marriage counselor, I have seen it all and heard it all. Both my work companions, in trouble with the females in their relationships, allowed me to talk some sense into their reprobate minds. A year later, we all worked together on the best of terms, and I commanded a well-earned respect from them.

Early in 2011, the peak-shaving facility contract came to a close. The general manager suggested I join their latest job in Northern Alberta's "oil patch," where a large refinery required an extensive refurbish of one of its plants. The four-month contract required an experienced material coordinator, but it meant I would work away from home for the first time. This job resulted in a succession of three more contracts, all in the same area, and a few months before my sixty-ninth birthday, I retired from the workforce.

While in Northern Alberta, I reviewed much of my Christian walk and time spent in the ministry. It surprised me to feel a great deal of mental conflict over the tenets of a religion that, up to the point of disillusionment, monopolized a great deal of my life. My entire past experience appeared to have been spent in pursuit of a bubble that always floated just out of my reach. For a few of the years that followed my retirement the past quest to serve God appeared as a wasted effort on a non-reality. My four-decade pursuit ended with a string of disappointments, broken relationships, and a sense of loss, all harbingers that fed an already depressed state of mind.

The Bigger Picture

With the emergence, however, of the bigger picture a new day began to dawn for me; a new revelation that helped me make sense of the religious landscape and its disconnect from reality. There is and always has been a place for a belief in God for those who like me, are so disposed; but if we rely on ancient views, then we need to take care that we interpret matters in the correct way. When people go as far as to proselyte others to their way of belief, the process of self-enlightenment can become disrupted. In 1 John 2:27 the word informs us:

"And you, the anointing you have received from Him (God) abides in you and you have no need that anyone should teach you…"

Father Richard Rohr of The Center for Action and Contemplation said in one of his daily meditation reflections: "All religious language is metaphor by necessity."

In a literal interpretation of scripture the process of real discovery is eliminated due to the metaphoric nature of the texts; but if that is how you like it, then follow your heart. If, on the other hand, you want to embrace the realities that metaphors teach, then the bigger picture will fit right into your wheelhouse. Each journey made by a diligent seeker will have its reward. I am uplifted by the fact that my belief system walks hand in hand with modern discovery, much of which can be discerned through the many metaphoric pictures penned in ancient scripture and revealed in the factual realities of modern science.

There is one more question relative to the bigger picture that requires an answer:

How do I relate to this new concept of an infinite Creator?

Worship and prayer are the two most common practices Christians use to relate to the God of the Bible. The idea of prayer and worship comes from Abraham's time (about 2400 BCE), when Abraham used his son, Isaac as a potential sacrifice. The "Law of First Use" suggested the element of sacrifice as the focal point of worship, but it has changed in practice over the years. The young shepherd boy, David, introduced a musical instrument to turn psalms into songs for the relaxation of King Solomon, a practice which became the forerunner of modern church worship. Now we have the involvement of many instruments, worship leaders, choir singers and bands that have hijacked the original concept and made it into a regular precursor to most church services. In the book of Romans Chapter 12: 1, we learn that we are to offer our bodies as a living sacrifice to God because that is our true worship (reasonable service). The church has picked up on the singing of praises to music as the required need for finding intimacy with God, a practice that prepares the mind for a spiritual encounter; but in reality, the spectacle of it all can detract from any sort of intimacy with the Lord. The original idea behind worship lay in the act of sacrifice, and points in metaphoric terms to how we live our lives and treat others.

To sacrifice the need of egotistical gratification is the true form of worship, and displays the embodiment of the Creator's love. I doubt worship in the form of a verbal practice carries any redemption qualities but rather impinges on the true nature of spiritual growth. It is rather the sacrifice of love from our hearts in an act of kindness towards others that is the true act of worship. I understand that true worship (for me) is to be the best person I can be, especially in difficult circumstances, and I do this in service to others. This is one of the aspects of the Law of One that I really appreciate, because we are told that the Creator would have us share His love even when the recipients do not deserve it. This is what it means to worship.

I am constantly aware of the indwelling presence of God, who occupies every molecule of my body and every thought of my mind. There is no need for me to express my love to the Creator in verbal terms, because love becomes obvious in my reactions to my family and to all the creatures of creation. Love and worship are also expressed in the way I treat my environment. Our need to find affirmation on the human level (with one another) is a human trait, not a godly one, and God does not need my lip service; he desires the service that comes as a natural reaction to those around me, and that comes from my heart. This is true worship.

Prayer hosts a similar tone. True prayer is as Jesus described it to his disciples, not about the vain repetitions made by the heathen, not asking for things you think you need, because God already knows what you need (Matthew 6: 7-8). As previously discussed, the Creator has made every provision in spacetime to accommodate our needs. A breakdown of what Jesus told his disciples is as follows; (Matthew 6: 9-12):

Acknowledge in your mind that God is to be respected and revered.

Understand that God's will is the best for all creation.

Be thankful for the provisions that make life livable.

Be mindful of God's forgiveness, and know that there is a correlation to the forgiveness you have shown to others. (Especially when they didn't deserve it.)

Know that within your higher self exists the enlightenment that will help you navigate temptation.

Jesus did not mean for this prayer model to become a standard cliché or a template for asking favors. Prayer is a process, done in secret; in the confines of one's mind:

The Bigger Picture

"But you, when you pray, enter into your room, and when you have shut the door pray to your Father who is in the secret place..." (Matthew 6:6).

I believe this refers to a metaphoric communication of the "two selves": between your higher and lower self (your mind).

We also need to ask the question: why would an all-powerful, all-knowing, and omnipresent God require us to worship Him? Do we think that God is so insecure that he requires a constant accolade of adoration from His followers? I think not. The Creator, I believe, is satisfied with our love, and that love is expressed in our relationships with His other creatures and the stewardship of this beautiful planet.

*

Thus ends The Bigger Picture: One Man's Journey from Religious Fundamentalism to Reality. Live in peace and be of assistance to all who need you; resist the inclination toward thoughts of violence. Above everything else, entertain the love of the One Infinite Creator in your heart and mind. Also, treat your environment with the respect it deserves; we only have one Earth.

—Colin

Notes

NB. Some of the definitions outlined below may not reflect mainstream scientific or philosophic parameters.

Introduction

1 Sumerian Civilization. A civilization of Southern Mesopotamia known today as modern Iraq that existed and flourished about 6000 years ago. The Sumerians were the first to use a writing technique called cuneiform. They also developed an instrument for financial exchange that became the forerunner to our modern checking system. They also had the first known standing army.

2 Reality. For the purpose of this treatise, Reality is the actual experience of all events, actions, reactions, and relationships, both historic and current. Reality is the outworking of worldly systems and the effects these have on personal and corporate living.

Chapter 1

3 The Union Of South Africa came into being on 31 May 1910, a few years after the war between the British and the Boers. The Union incorporated the provinces of Natal, Cape, Transvaal and the Orange River colonies (known as the Orange Free State). The Union began a self-governing dominion under the British Empire, but became a Republic on 31st May 1961.

4 The Creator of our Universe. Creation Theory is the fundamental foundation of the many religions that have formed since

the earliest times of civilization. The theory surmises that a deity (God) brought the universe into being through a divine act of creation. Atheists and agnostics dispute this, citing a lack of material proof, and conclude that the origin of the cosmos cannot be known. Creationists, however, believe that causality is the smoking gun for belief in a deity. They feel it is preferable to live with a known cause, even if that cause is contestable and requires the element of faith to make it believable; the argument of what preceded the universe ends with the concept of a divine Creator and therefore solves the need for any further preceding process.

5 The principal of a High school. M.L. Sultan Technical College, situated in Durban, of which the high school served as a subsidiary, received a financial boost through a large sum in 1941 donated by Malukmahomed Lappa Sultan for the purpose of educating the growing immigrant Indian population of KwaZulu-Natal. Laborers, who possessed little or no education, were brought from India in the 1800's to work in the sugar cane industry of Natal.

Chapter 2

6 Military Conscription. Recruitment on a voluntary basis of white South African males for the purpose of fielding a viable army in the event of further wars. Conscription started in 1912 while South Africa was still a Union. Up to 1967, recruitment remained voluntary, after which time parliament introduced a system of conscription, and made it mandatory for all white, male citizens. Members served in the South African Defense Force with a choice to remain as a civilian conscript or join the permanent force, and periods of service ranged from three months in the early years to twenty-four months in later years. Conscription ended in 1993.

7 Swimming Pool Endeavor. The author started a swimming pool construction company under the name of Permacrete Con-

struction, which he later sold without any assets. Several years of building experience had been gained while building pools for Blue Lake Penguin Pools in Durban.

8 Afrikaans. A language, derivative from Dutch, that became one of the official languages of South Africa. The Dutch, under Jan Van Riebeek, arrived at the Cape to set up the Dutch East India Trading Company in 1641. Both English and Afrikaans were taught as official languages in South African schools until the regime change in 1994. Since that time, nine more official languages have been added: Sotho, Tsonga, Tswana, Tswana, Swati, Zulu, Ndebele, Xhosa, and Venda.

9 Fundamentalist, Conservative, Evangelical. The word "fundamentalist" has a religious connotation to it and alludes to a belief system that is based on ancient scripture, which is followed by converts, to the letter. The converts generally adhere to conservative ideology and partake in forms of evangelism with the aim to proselyte others.

10 Quakers. A religious movement that originally emerged in England during the 17th century and formally became known as the Friend's Church until the name "Quaker" was coined to label the movement. It is said that the founder, George Fox, told a magistrate to tremble whenever the name of God was mentioned, but another source says that it referred to the quaking motion of the members when they entered a religious experience.

11 King James English. It is the inclination of the Pentecostal groups to use Shakespearian English, the language of the King James Bible, to make their prayers, prophecies, and interpretation of tongues appear more austere and authoritative.

Chapter 3

12 Eternal Security. Also Known as "Perseverance of the Saints," or "Once saved, always saved." The doctrine evolved out of the teachings of John Calvin and advocates that once a soul has been regenerated by God through the power of the Holy Spirit, the condition is irreversible.

13 Pentecostal Church. The Pentecostal movement is based on the experience of the Baptism in the Holy Spirit that took place in the "upper room," where 120 people were gathered for a time of prayer. It was referred to as the Day of Pentecost. The Holy Spirit fell upon the group and many spoke in tongues (Acts 2:1-4). The first outbreak of modern Pentecostalism was in January of 1901. The advent spawned a movement that swept the twentieth-century Christian world.

14 Falling away from the faith. The passage in Hebrews 6: 4-6 is primarily used to support the doctrine of falling away from the faith, and is in conflict with the doctrine of Eternal Security. Advocates maintain that believers can fall away from the faith through backsliding and sin.

15 The Chosen. There are many scriptures in the Bible that refer to the "called of God" or "chosen," an interpretation of scripture called Predestination. The advocates believe that God chose certain people before the foundations of the world and only these people will be saved.

Chapter 4

16 Work Study. Following the Industrial Revolution, factories began to study the way work was being done in order to improve profitability. Time and motion study became the means of ascertaining the duration of all physical actions performed on the parts of manufactured material in the production process on the factory floor. It involved the balancing out of workstations on assembly lines and the timing of all repetitive operations in order to produce a labor cost, to which the cost of materials and

overheads were added. Work Study also involved workshop organization and management, production planning and control.

17 Ruling Political Party. In 1948, the Nationalist Party won the majority vote in the South African parliament and introduced most of the tenets of apartheid. It was made up mostly of Afrikaans-speaking citizens who were members of the Dutch Reformed Church.

Chapter 5

18 The Gideons. An organization of business and professional people who place Bibles in hotels, motels, and hospitals.

19 Youth for Christ. A worldwide Christian movement, started in 1946, working with young people.

20 Para-church organizations. Faith-based Christian organizations that work across denominational lines to promote faith in Christ.

Chapter 6

21 Particular operation. The project involved the dismantling of an entire plant in the main factory, situated in Durban, and its reassembly in the new location. The plant manufactured three-legged cooking pots through a molding process for export to African countries.

Chapter 7

22 400 Ton Press. A Hydraulic embossing press for the manufacture of sheet steel stove parts.

Chapter 8

23 Isometric drawings. Drawings that project a three-dimensional view in two-dimensional form. Thousands of feet of industrial piping with varying diameters were represented by the isometrics showing the welding requirements.

Chapter 9

24 KwaZulu-Natal. The domain of the Zulu nation residing in the province of Natal. It is home to the Nkatha Freedom Party, led by Chief Mangosuthu Buthelezi, under the Kingship of Goodwill Zwelithini.

Chapter 11

25 Living in the Metaphor. A metaphor is defined as a figure of speech that does not literally apply to the action or object being spoken of. "I have a mountain of work waiting for me." The work is not a literal mountain, but the word mountain paints a picture of a large workload. The Bible is laden with metaphoric language because it was written for all ages and societies.

Here is a classic metaphor in which Christians will rest their case for being a God- created being:
Yet you, Lord, are our Father.
We are the clay, you are the potter;
we are all the work of your hand. (Isa 64:8)
The metaphoric use of "Father", "clay", "potter", "work of your hand" paints a picture of God fashioning us with his hands as a potter uses clay to fashion a vase. The metaphor gives the impression that this is a direct hands-on creation of a person's body and soul. Unless one makes an effort to bring the verse to reflect its intended reality, the above impression will remain as a direct hands-on action. The reality, however, as science has proved, is that a process of evolution, which took billions of years, resulted in cells forming enough complexity to develop

into ape-like forms to become hominids and then (perhaps with the help of extraterrestrials) to become humans.

Chapter 23

26 The Law of Probability. Various sites that provide definitions give complicated answers for this theory. The author uses the law in the way described below:
There is a ratio that exists between the outcome of any event and incurs the intervention of variables, any of which may influence that outcome. Out of two possible results for an event, the eventual outcome would be either positive or negative. This is a 50/50 result. Should the number of outcomes increase due to greater variables being present, that ratio could change from 50/50 to, perhaps, 30/70 or 20/80.

Chapter 28

27 The Greek Septuagint or LXX. The earliest Greek translation of the original Hebrew scriptures. It contained the Torah (Pentateuch), the first five books of Hebrew Law.

28 Pharisee. A member of the Jewish sect that observed and taught the strict observance of Jewish law.

Chapter 30

29 Personality Type. Myers-Briggs is a personality type indicator. INFJ: I=Introverted; N=Intuitive; F=Feeling (Empathetic); J=Judging. INFJ's are very rare and makeup about one percent of a population. They tend to see their purpose in life is to help others.

Chapter 32

30 Quantum Physics. The study of microphysics. The mysterious behavior of subatomic particles, the smallest forms of matter, and the peculiar, dual aspect of the quantum wave. Particles entangled with each other and the existence of particles that can be in more than one place at the same time.

31 Entanglement or Superposition. The double-slit experiment: When a particle of light (a photon) is accelerated towards two side-by-side slits in a vertically held barrier, the photon takes both slits at the same time, which shows that the photon, while existing as a particle, is also in the form of a wave. As the photon exits both slits at the same time the two different parts of the wave interfere with each other and are said to be "entangled" or in a superposition. Entangled particles will retain a relationship no matter how far apart they move away from each other.

32 Hubble Space Telescope. Named after the astronomer, Edwin Hubble, it was the first space-based optical telescope to be deployed into orbit around the Earth. Hubble was launched from the space shuttle Discovery in April 1990.

33 Astrophysics. The study of the nature of celestial bodies through the use of the principles of physics and chemistry.

34 Astrobiology. The study of the origins and evolution of life in the Universe.

35 Exobiology. The study of the nature and possibility of life on other planets.

Chapter 36

36 Biocentrism. The concept of life and consciousness as the construction of reality. Dr. Robert Lanza's book, Biocentrism: the Key to Understanding the Universe, provides us with ideas

on how we relate to the universe. It paves the way for consciousness to be seen as an immortal essence of life.

37 Spacetime Continuum. The combination of the three dimensions of space and one dimension of time into a single entity that manifests in a continuous propagation of events.

Chapter 37

38 Causality. Everything must have a cause. There is no effect in the universe that was not caused by something.

Chapter 38

39 Exoplanets. Planets that may harbor life and are orbiting a star in another solar system. These planets are in the "Goldilocks region" of their star, which means they are at a distance which will allow liquid water to form and thereby, life, as we know it.

40 The Quantum link in Spacetime. It is been irrevocably proved that spacetime is an illusion to make us think everything is separated from everything else. The opposite is in fact true. All points in spacetime are connected, and we understand this from the "entanglement" of particles that, when in a superposition form can send information from an entangled particle to its "buddy" at a speed many times the speed of light, or instantaneously. Scientists are working on this process to link it to travel.

41 Consciousness. Consciousness is thought to be the progenitor of movement from one place in the universe to another. If the quantum conscious state creates all our reality, then it may also be the solution to travel from one point in space to another.

42 Energy from the Quantum Vacuum (or Zero Point Energy). It is believed that quantum fluctuations in the space vacuum are a source of free energy.

43 The Military Industrial Complex. The industrial companies tasked with the development of many Government black-ops projects that involve the very latest technologies secured from downed UFOs (like the Roswell incident).

Chapter 39

44 The Ra Group. The Ra group are a society of benevolent extraterrestrials who have made contact with humans on Earth in an effort to help with the business of disclosure. They are believed to be of the Blue Avian group and are a part of the Intergalactic Federation of planets that exist in the Milky Way galaxy. The Ra believe they have been sent to help the humans of Earth to understand the way the universe works and are the bearers of the Law of One material.

45 Sixth Density Collective social memory Complex assembly of Extraterrestrials. According to the Law of One, all universal jurisdictions are divided into eight densities (an octave). The densities may be seen as differing vibratory dimensions that exist in parallel to support many different species of beings. The Earth consists of three vibratory levels (or densities), of which humans are on the third level. The transition from one dimension to the next is a matter of responding to the different vibrations through consciousness.

Manufactured by Amazon.ca
Bolton, ON